In this fresh and engaging treatment of Luke/Acts, Luuk van de Weghe contributes meaningfully to our understandings of biblical historiography regarding the histories of early Christianity and Jesus of Nazareth. By excavating five distinctive features of Luke's two volumes … the author not only argues for Luke's use of eyewitness testimony; he demonstrates how this was done. In the light of this analysis, Luke 1.2 comes into lucid focus. Appreciation for what he has received from 'eyewitnesses and servants of the word' is not just a throwaway line; it reflects the epistemological character of much of Luke's material.

Paul N. Anderson
Author of *The Christology of the Fourth Gospel, The Fourth Gospel and the Quest for Jesus,* and *From Crisis to Christ: A Contextual Introduction to the New Testament*

The Historical Tell is a short book and yet it packs a strong punch. Luuk van de Weghe relies upon some classic arguments, but arranges them in a unique fashion, and adds some new insights as to why there is eyewitness testimony behind Luke and Acts.

Sean McDowell
Professor of Apologetics, Biola University
Author or co-author of multiple books including
Evidence that Demands a Verdict

Luuk van de Weghe would make an excellent detective. In *The Historical Tell,* he carefully sifts through the data from the Gospel of Luke and the Book of Acts, searching for evidence of eyewitness testimony. His discoveries bolster the case for the reliability of the New

Testament from several unique investigative angles. If you're interested in an engaging evidential approach to the case for Jesus, *The Historical Tell* will inspire and encourage you. I highly recommend it.

J. Warner Wallace
Dateline featured Cold-Case Detective
Senior Fellow at the Colson Center for Christian Worldview
Adjunct Professor of Apologetics at Talbot School of Theology
Author of *Cold-Case Christianity* and *Person of Interest*

This book is a rare accomplishment: van de Weghe succeeds in condensing for a popular audience a vast amount of scholarly research directly relevant to understanding Luke-Acts. Popular readers will enjoy a presentation brimming with lively examples from history and modern culture while scholars will value the substantial analysis supported by original research, full endnotes, and appendices. Anyone interested in understanding how the eyewitnesses functioned as sources in the writing of Luke and Acts needs to reckon with van de Weghe's work.

John J. Peters
Author of *Luke Among the Ancient Historians*

On the question of the historical reliability of Luke-Acts, Luuk van de Weghe breaks some new ground. Most important is his meticulous analysis of names, demonstrating that here Luke is in line with serious historians like Plutarch, Suetonius, or Josephus. Vivid details, especially in the Lukan special material, point to the memories of eye-witnesses. Very stimulating is the author's explanation of the parallels between the Gospels of Luke and John. The study strengthens the view that Luke was not third-generation believer but could himself interrogate eyewitnesses of the Jesus story.

Rainer Riesner
Professor emeritus of New Testament
University of Dortmund, Germany

I have previewed this book with great interest, admiration, and, dare I say, envy. The author displays to me an incredible breadth of authoritative knowledge.... This is not a book of many pages, but that should not obscure the huge investment in the depth and skill of the author's research.

Paul Barnett
Lecturer Emeritus, Moore Theological College
Author of *Is the New Testament Reliable?*

THE HISTORICAL TELL

The Historical Tell

Patterns of Eyewitness Testimony in the Gospel of Luke and Acts

Luuk van de Weghe

DeWard
for your journey

To my daughters:

Suzy, Elsie, June, Maggie, and Wendy.

Thanks for all the gray hair and the loads of fun.

Contents

Foreword 7

Acknowledgements 9

Abbreviations 11

Introduction 15

1. Upping the Ante 22

2. Unintentional Byproduct 31

3. Closer and Earlier 37

4. The Mechanism 42

5. Intention 48

6. To Tell It Like the Scriptures 83

7. After the *Achterhuis* 63

8. Convergence 71

9. The Beloved Eyewitness 82

10. Acceptable 87

11. Majestic 98

12. Theography 104

Conclusion 111

Appendix A: Personal Names in Comparable Sources 115

Appendix B: Semitisms Unique to Luke-Acts 124

Endnotes 140

Index 177

Foreword

It is a given in New Testament scholarship that Luke and Acts is one work separated by the limitation of weight and size of a single scroll. No agreement, however, is held about the historical worth of this text.

This is a significant issue. Without Luke and Acts there is no way of knowing how the Jesus of the Gospels related to the early church as reflected in the letters of Paul, Peter, John, and the Letter to the Hebrews. Luke and Acts, which chronicles the seven decades between the birth of John the Baptist and Paul's arrival and early imprisonment in Rome, is the bridge between Jesus of Nazareth and the church.

A case could be made, therefore, that historically speaking, Luke and Acts is the most important text within the corpus of the New Testament. It certainly is the most voluminous, representing about twenty-five percent of the New Testament.

Luke and Acts has its critics, but also its defenders, including such authorities as Martin Hengel, F.F. Bruce, Colin Hemer, Craig Keener, and recently, Daniel J-S Chae.[1] To those names can now be added Luuk van de Weghe.

I have previewed this book with great interest, admiration, and, dare I say, envy. The author displays to me an incredible breadth of authoritative knowledge—names, cultural details, minute observations…the list goes on. Van de Weghe employs the notion of a "tell," that is, of involuntary facial signals card players give as noted by their competitors. His argument is that many details in Luke and Acts send such messages to its readers, that is, to sharp-eyed readers like the author.

Five "tells" direct the study—Luke's use of names; his patterns of vivid detail (focusing on his narrative of the sea voyage to Rome); his clustering of language to highlight eyewitness testimony; his patterns of adapting received texts, for example, Mark's; and his patterns of connectivity between the Gospels of Luke and John.

Several features stand out. One is his extensive footnoting of Graeco-Roman texts relating to eyewitness reporting and how important this was in ancient historiography. The author's own commitment to evidence-based inquiry matches the diligence and high ideals of the author of Luke and Acts. His scholarship in ancient writings has served his research to a high degree.

Another is his interest in the names of people that appear within Luke and Acts. He explores the notion of the names of people and the contexts in which those names appear. Thanks to vast resources of onomastic scholarship Van de Weghe has studied hundreds of names that appear in New Testament texts, apocryphal writings, ancient biographies, and fiction. The materials appended are evidence of significant investment of time and reflection.

One other feature attracted my attention: the author's awareness of the phenomenon of memory, and the elements that cement details into memory.

This is not a book of many pages, but that should not obscure the huge investment in the depth and skill of the author's research.

Paul Barnett, Ph.D., Th.D. (hon)
Lecturer Emeritus, Moore Theological College

Acknowledgements

I would like to thank Cambridge University Press and Tyndale House, Cambridge, for allowing the republication of material from *New Testament Studies* and the *Tyndale Bulletin* within various chapters of this book, and I am thankful to the anonymous reviewers and to the editors of these journals, as well as to Dr. Paul Barnett, for sharpening my research and writing. Christopher Lensch, Dr. John Battle, and Dr. Tomas Bokedal—your academic mentorship throughout my graduate and postgraduate studies at Western Reformed Seminary and the University of Aberdeen has been invaluable. I owe a great debt to my parents, Rob and Jacoba van de Weghe. Their piety and analytical thinking have shaped me as a person and as a student of the New Testament. My appreciation also goes out to Nathan Ward for his flexibility and his after-hours efforts in bringing this project to completion. Lastly, I would like to thank my wife, Sandy, for her endless support, her thoughtful feedback, and her countless sacrifices that made this book possible.

Abbreviations

ABD	*Anchor Bible Dictionary*
AnBib	*Analecta Biblica*
ANRW	*Aufstieg und Niedergang der römischen Welt*
ATI	*American Theological Inquiry*
BETL	Bibliotheca Ephemeridum Theologicarum Lovaniensium
Bib	*Biblica*
BibAn	*The Biblical Annals*
BBR	*Bulletin for Biblical Research*
BECNT	Baker Exegetical Commentary on the New Testament
BMSEC	Baylor-Mohr Siebeck Studies in Early Christianity
BZNW	Beihefte zur Zeitschrift für die Neutestamentliche Wissenschaft
CBQ	*Catholic Biblical Quarterly*
CIIP	*Corpus Inscriptionum Iudaeae/Palaestinae*
DPRR	Digital Prosopography of the Roman Republic
GRBS	*Greek, Roman, and Byzantine Studies*
HA-ESI	Hadashot Arkheologiyot—Excavations and Surveys in Israel
HTKNT	Herders theologischer Kommentar zum Neuen Testament
HTR	*Harvard Theological Review*
Ilan I	*Lexicon of Jewish Names in Late Antiquity: Part 1: Palestine 330 BCE—200 CE*
JBL	*Journal of Biblical Literature*

JETS	*Journal of the Evangelical Theological Society*
JGRChJ	*Journal of Greco-Roman Christianity and Judaism*
JSHJ	*Journal for the Study of the Historical Jesus*
JSNT	*Journal for the Study of the New Testament*
JSNTSup	Journal for the Study of the New Testament: Supplement Series
JTS	*Journal of Theological Studies*
LGPN	*Lexicon of Greek Personal Names*
LXX	Septuagint
MSS	Manuscripts
NovT	*Novum Testamentum*
NTS	*New Testament Studies*
OPTAT	*Occasional Papers in Translation and Textlinguistics*
PIR	*Prosopographia Imperii Romani*
ProsPtol	*Prosopographia Ptolemaica*
RBL	*Review of Biblical Literature*
RevBib	*Revue Biblique*
RSR	*Religious Studies Review*
SBFA	Studium Biblicum Franciscanum Analecta
SNTSMS	Society of New Testament Studies Monograph Series
SNTU	Studien zum Neuen Testament und seiner Umwelt
TAPhA	*Transactions and Proceedings of the American Philological Association*
TynBul	*Tyndale Bulletin*
THGNT	Tyndale House Greek New Testament
TLG	Thesaurus Linguae Graecae
TSAJ	Texte und Studien zum antiken Judentum
WUNT	Wissenschaftliche Untersuchungen zum Neuen Testament

ZDVP	*Zeitschrift des deutschen Piilastina-Vereins*
ZPE	*Zeitschrift für Papyrologie und Epigraphik*

Introduction

As with the Dutchman, so with the Christian. A Dutchman understands his country in two ways. The first way is through his heart. He passes through its tulip fields, rides his bike through its streets, experiences its culture from within. His life is part of its history. The Netherlands is a truth experienced. A place called home. The second way is intellectual. He pinpoints his country on a map. He reads its history in a textbook. He talks facts. Cerebral facts. Dispassionate truths.

As with the Dutchman, so with the Christian. Christianity can be lived out, but it also rings true. It visits us in the present, but it has its roots in the past. For the Christian, all spiritual experience is in some sense anchored in the historical life of one person. This person had followers, and these followers shared their experiences with those who would listen. As we will see, the author of Luke's Gospel claimed be such a listener. He believed that the past events of Jesus' life deserve remembrance. Luke's message was defined by the past more than a country is defined by its borders. When we consider the historical foundations of Luke's text, we honor him and the one of whom he wrote.

The Gospel of Luke is like the masterpiece we have found in the attic. We have long wondered whether some illustrious painter produced it. It has long appeared valuable to us. At some point we owe to ourselves to have it authenticated, although the authentication process of a painting is costly. As with the painting, so with the Gospel of Luke. Historical research offers neither certainty nor glory. It offers only hints and patterns and probabilities. It can be cold and lifeless. Yet, out of this coldness, it can also surprise us with truth. It may be coy, but it does not lie.

This brings us to the method we will employ in our authentication process of Luke's Gospel and some relevant portions of the book of Acts.† In their 2003 article, "Cues to Deception," Bella DePaulo and her colleagues discuss the latest research into how liars behave during person-to-person dialogues.[2] Their analysis suggests that no single behavior always occurs when people lie. Instead, certain cues *generally* accompany deception more often than they accompany honesty, and vice versa.[3] The following patterns, according to their study, form cues to honesty and deception:

- Truthtellers are generally more informative and detailed in their accounts.[4]
- Liars' tales are generally less plausible than truthful accounts and lack the immediacy and personal engagement of truthtellers' versions.[5]
- Liars' accounts contain less normal imperfections and unusual details, likely resulting from prior rehearsal or from a need to "stick to the script."[6]

In poker, certain types of subtle cues, especially patterns of unique mannerisms, are called "tells." These are signals that reveal a player's bluff and give away the truth about their hand. Merriam-Webster gives the following entries for "tell" (noun):

---

†The book of Acts, the sequel to Luke's Gospel, focuses primarily on the growth of the early church and the missionary work of Peter and Paul. With most scholars, I assume that the author of Acts and the author of Luke's Gospel are the same person. For a terrific overview of scholarly positions regarding the unity of Luke and Acts, see Michael Bird, "The Unity of Luke-Acts in Recent Discussion," *JSNT* 29.4 (2007), pp. 425–448.

1. An inadvertent behavior or mannerism that betrays a poker player's true thoughts, intentions, or emotions

"The World Series of Poker: earth's greatest liars gathered together with millions of dollars on the line … It's a blur of action, but the educated spectator ignores these distractions and focuses on the players' mannerisms—it's all part of the science of *tells*, reflexes a player can't control that, read right, give away his thoughts."

—Seth Stevenson

2. A revealing gesture, expression, etc., that is likened to a poker player's tell

"But his eyes darted fractionally to one side as he said it …; the classic liar's *tell*."

– Stephen King

broadly: SIGN, INDICATION

"I talked to staffers who said that their bosses had two or three flights booked getting out of town, a big *tell* that there was not going to be a deal."

—Kelly O'Donnell

A tell does not always reveal deception. As Merriam-Webster's second entry indicates, the term can be neutral. A tell generally has two characteristics. First, it is subtle. Second, it generally—but not always—occurs as a *pattern* of behavior.

Throughout this book, we will treat Luke the Evangelist like any other person making a claim—not so different, say, from a homeowner making a claim on an insurance policy or a suspect in a criminal case making a claim to innocence. We are not going to assume anything about him that the church has told us.[7] We are not going to assume that he is trustworthy. Instead, we will test him. Can his claims be verified? Is he reliable? We will seek an answer to these questions by looking at Luke's "tells." That is, we are going to see if there are deeper patterns under the surface of his text that indicate what his writings reveal about him as a historian. This project will demand a certain meticulousness, but its reward will be great. It will demonstrate that Luke's interest in going back to the sources, his interest in inquiring of those who saw and spoke with Jesus, is more than a claim Luke makes. Some of Luke's tells are especially significant because they would be extremely hard to mimic for someone *not* writing an authentic account but particularly difficult *to avoid creating* for someone who is.

We are going to approach the clues that Luke leaves much like detectives coming onto a crime scene. Each piece of evidence needs to be examined not only for its own explanatory value, but also for how it works with other pieces of evidence to paint a picture of the truth. Luke's historical tells are not like a single clue but rather weave together to create the very fabric of his composition. They build upon one another in layers that we will peel away in this investigation. First, however, we should ask the question: what are Luke's claims as a historian?

Luke's Claims

The clearest assertion Luke makes about his own project is contained in the preface to his Gospel (Luke 1.1–4):

Ἐπειδήπερ πολλοὶ ἐπεχείρησαν ἀνατάξασθαι διήγησιν περὶ τῶν πεπληροφορημένων ἐν ἡμῖν πραγμάτων, [2] καθὼς παρέδοσαν ἡμῖν οἱ ἀπ᾽ ἀρχῆς αὐτόπται καὶ ὑπηρέται γενόμενοι τοῦ λόγου, [3] ἔδοξε κἀμοὶ παρηκολουθηκότι ἄνωθεν πᾶσιν ἀκριβῶς καθεξῆς σοι γράψαι, κράτιστε Θεόφιλε, [4] ἵνα ἐπιγνῷς περὶ ὧν κατηχήθης λόγων τὴν ἀσφάλειαν.[8]

Since many have tried to tell the whole story of the things accomplished among us [2] in light of [the accounts] that the early eyewitnesses (who became devoted to the message) delivered to us, [3] it seemed good for me especially, having had an informed familiarity with everything for a long time, to write to you in such a way, most excellent Theophilus, [4] that you might know the reliability of the accounts you have been taught.[9]

A recent study by John Peters rekindles the suggestion that Luke 1.2 refers to *living* eyewitnesses who delivered (παρέδοσαν—active, not passive, contra NIV, NRSV) accounts to Luke.[10] The preface quoted above, likewise, places Luke within the traditions of the great Fathers of History: Thucydides (b. 460 BCE) and Herodotus (b. 484 BCE). In line with these traditions, Luke's prologue stresses the themes of inquiry, "autopsy," (of "seeing for oneself," not to be confused with the modern term), careful investigation/informed familiarity, and a concern with "beginnings" (cf. Herodotus 1.5.3; Thucydides 1.23.4).[11] In the book of Acts, Luke—like other historians (cf. Diodorus 1.4.1; Dion. Halic., *Ant. Rom.* 1.1.2; Josephus, *B.J.* 1.16)—also seems to take an interest in travel.[12]

This last issue was especially important to ancient historians within the Thucydidean heritage. Such historians believed that only through autopsy and the inquiry of living witnesses could true historical research be achieved for recent events.[13] Polybius—a Greek historian of the second century BCE—believed, for example, that inquiry was the most important duty of a historian (12.4.4c). Even Herodotus, although he was less rigid than Thucydides in his concern for accuracy, once traveled to Thasos and Tyre to research a single point (2.44, cf. 2.102).[14] Importantly, within the broad Greco-Roman tradition of history writing, this ideal of experiential testimony—whether through an author's direct participation or via the inquiry of eyewitnesses—led many ancient historians to see the act of writing history as appropriate only for events that could be investigated in person.[15] After all, it was only under such circumstances that living memory could remain accessible. Across the spectrum of Roman historical writings (e.g., Caesar, *B.G.* 1.50.4, 5.18.4, 2.15.3; Velleius 2.101.2–3; Ammianus 15.1.1; Eutropius 10.16; Sallust, *Cat.* 48.9; Tacitus, *Ann.* 1.61.2; etc.) the most validating source was the abiding source, the participant/eyewitness, whether that be the author himself or his informant, to which John Marincola, a specialist in Greek and Roman historiography, remarks, "there is no reason to think the Roman historians valued inquiry based on participation any less than did the Greek."[16] If we take these observations back into Luke's preface, it leads us to expect that Luke was claiming *not* to have merely read the accounts of others but to have *inquired of living eyewitnesses* who were present from the beginning of Jesus' ministry.[17]

This brings us to the focus of our present study. In this concise book, we will investigate a singular question: *did Luke rely on eyewitness testimony?* We will argue that Luke's use of eyewitness testimony is consistent with his historical tells and that it often provides the best explanation for their presence. Moreso, we will argue that these tells create *a corroborative evidence case* in favor of Luke's use of eyewitness testimony.[18]

This argument is not merely what one would call "cumulative," like a rope made up of many strands. It is corroborative. That is, every piece of evidence not merely strengthens the overall case, but often also corroborates—that is, strengthens—another piece of evidence at the same time. It is as if, while adding another strand onto a rope, a piece of thread also gets tangled up with another strand to make it thicker.

We could use a criminal case to illustrate the distinction. Demonstrating that a suspect had both motive and opportunity to commit a crime strengthens the case that the suspect is guilty, but neither element in the case increases the probative strength of the other. Nevertheless, they form part of a cumulative case towards the suspect's guilt.

New let us take a case in which a set of independent witnesses testify that they each saw the suspect commit the crime. In the process, they provide incidental details that line up with one another's testimonies. This set of witnesses also increases the likelihood of the suspect's guilt, but their testimony is more than cumulative; not only do their testimonies confirm the guilt of the suspect, but their testimonies, in the process, strengthen the reliability of the other independent witnesses by corroborating their accounts.[19] I will provide some specific examples of how Luke's tells accomplish this at the end of the next chapter.

This corroborative evidence case is established in our first nine chapters. A second conclusion of our study is that Luke's use of eyewitness testimony and his literary creativity can be seen as complementary as opposed to contradictory. This topic is discussed in our last three chapters. The search for Luke's tells is especially fitting because Luke, like other historians writing in the tradition of Thucydides, discusses his use of sources in his preface but subtly conceals his reliance upon them in his narrative.[20]

ONE

Upping the Ante

Throughout our study, we will examine five tells to determine the likelihood that Luke relied on eyewitness testimony. Several tells are patterns that occur within Luke's text. Are these consistent with Luke's use of eyewitness sources? These could be compared to, say, the consistency of a suspect's testimony over time or the way it fulfills expectations of what it ought to appear/sound like. Other tells function more like corroborating pieces of evidence, such as additional testimony, for example, or fingerprint evidence. These do not necessarily occur independently, side by side, but as we will see, can be layered on top of one another.

Five Tells

Here I introduce Luke's five tells in the order that we will discuss them in this book.

Tell 1—Patterns of Names

First, we will look at Luke's use of names. Others have researched this topic before, but we will build on their work extensively and refine it. The topic of names may seem insignificant, and that is precisely the point. These are the types of details I referred to in the Introduction, those which are extremely hard to mimic for someone *not* writing an authentic account but particularly difficult *to avoid creating* for someone who is.

The power of this tell lies in the precision of patterns. It is not about a single name being used correctly or not; it is about a statistical pattern of correct names in a text. Nevertheless, I want to focus here on a single example to illustrate the *type* of detail I might consider when it comes to names.

Imagine trying to create a believable story about a trip taken to the U.S. in the early 2000s. How would you refer to Barack Obama? President Obama, if it's 2008? sSenator Obama, if it's 2002 and you are politically savvy enough to know the senator from Illinois? In this example, the names (or titles) we give to President Obama are dependent on the time in history.

But what if we lived during Jesus' time, when multiple languages were spoken in ancient Palestine? Details like the variation of names used could provide clues to the origin of information related to the language the provider of information spoke. To give you a brief sample—and it occurs in a very small detail—a scholar named Richard Fellows observes that Mariam (Μαριάμ), the Semitic (i.e., Hebrew/Aramaic) variant of Mary's name, occurs in all of Luke and Matthew's texts when they refer to Jesus' mother.[21] This form, Mariam, would have been how Aramaic-speaking Jews like Peter, Andrew, and Mary Magdalene would have likely referred to her.

There are, however, two exceptions to this Semitic usage of Mary's name in Luke's writings. The first exception is in Acts 1.14, where Luke uses the Greek variant of Mary's name, Μαρία (Maria). Fellows conjectures reasonably that Luke here uses the form of Mary's name that *Luke himself* would have been accustomed to using. It is the Greek form, after all, and there continues to be a strongly held belief that Luke was a Gentile author.[22] Likewise,

Luke's Greek audience would likely be familiar with the Greek version of Mary's name, Μαρία, that Luke uses here in Acts 1.14.

The other occurrence of this Greek form of Mary's name, very relevant to the question we are asking in our study on eyewitness testimony, is Luke 2.19: "And Μαρία (Maria) treasured up these things, pondering them in her heart."[23] This is the only occurrence of Mary's name in Luke's Gospel within the context of her personal reflections. Its form, like the form in Acts 1.14, is Greek and not Semitic. This indeed, as Fellows suggest, lends credence to the idea that this comment is not part of any written or oral tradition Luke may have received, since the other traditional material we have retains the Semitic form of her name.[24] Instead, when Luke writes that "Mary (Greek form) treasured up all these things…" he uses the form of her name that *he* would have been accustomed to using in-person. In this case, this minute detail, this particular form of Mary's name, increases the probability that Luke gleaned this information from a personal encounter rather than from a broader stock tradition.[25]

Does this prove that Luke personally received this information from an eyewitness source? No, it does not. Similarly, no single twitch of the eye or purse of the lips indicates the type of hand that a poker player might have. Rather, these can form part of a larger pattern. As we look at Luke's usage of names later, we will look especially at large-scale patterns of names, what they tell us about the Gospels generally, and specifically what they tell us about the writings of Luke.

Tell 2—Patterns of Vivid Detail

Second, we will look at patterns of vivid detail in a specific account from the book of Acts and see how this relates to what we would expect from someone who is relating a firsthand experience. This is important because if Luke is recording his firsthand experiences in the book of Acts as a traveling companion of Paul, it places him in the proximity of eyewitnesses to the life of Jesus. This tell relies on a pattern of vivid detail, but sometimes even a single description or item can be significant. A good example of such a detail is this description of Nazareth in Luke 4.29: "They got up, drove him [Jesus] out of the town, and took him to the brow of the hill on which the town was built, in order to throw him off the cliff."

This verse indicates not only that Nazareth was built upon a hill but upon a hill with a certain precipice (the ὀφρύος, or "eyebrow" of the hill) steep and high enough to throw someone from; it also appears to be a local description and quite a remarkable one if it could be verified. Recently, an archaeologist named Yardenna Alexandre published a report from her 2009/2011 excavations in central Nazareth.[26] Alexandre discovered the remains of a house that by the time of Jesus would have been situated in a small hamlet with an area of approximately 150 by 250 yards, centered over the current Franciscan Compound and bordered on the East by the modern Paulus VI road.[27] Early Roman Nazareth would have been an obscure, out-the-way settlement, in accord with the impression given by Nathanael's comment recorded in John 1.46: "Can anything good come from Nazareth?"

When I saw her pictures of modern-day Nazareth, I did not see any cliffs in the vicinity and assumed that Luke might have made an error. Having contacted Dr. Alexandre about her findings and the nature of the description of Luke 4.29, I was assured that the old village was indeed built into the hills, likely over the Compound, as just discussed, but that although the Paulus VI road now hides the precipice, many yards of fill were brought in to raise it during the developments of the mid-twentieth century.[28] Given the small, obscure nature of Nazareth with no extra-biblical references until the third century CE, it appears that Luke expresses a specific, local, accurate feature of topography. But whom could Luke get this information from if he did not receive it—at least indirectly—from the relatives of Jesus who lived in this small village? We will look for those small details and analyze them as evidence in our investigation.

Tell 3—Patterns of Style

Luke's third tell is a pattern of biblical style that runs through the Greek text of his Gospel. Luke literately crafts certain portions of his text to sound like the Septuagint.[†] Our investigation will uncover that Luke clusters his biblical language–mimicking the Septuagint—around portions of text that also bear features of eyewitness testimony, as if to highlight these sections.

This is suggestive because this was not just a case of giving these accounts a "biblical flavor." We must keep in mind that the biblical scrolls of the Jews living in the time of Jesus were perhaps the most sacred objects in their possession; they set the Jewish people apart. This was especially true after the destruction of the temple in 70 CE (the time at which Luke likely was writing). Not only is the importance of the sacred Scriptures consistently affirmed in Jewish and early Christian sources, but two specific instances from antiquity highlight the knowledge of this fact even among the Romans. The first is an instance wherein a Roman soldier tore up some biblical scrolls amid a conflict with the Jews (Josephus, *Ant.* 20.5.4); consequently, the Jews demanded restitution so forcefully that the regional governor Cumanus ordered the soldier to be beheaded just to squelch the uprising. The second example comes from 66 CE when the Jews were fleeing Caesarea (Josephus, *B.J.* 2.14.5–6). During their flight, they gathered

---

[†]The Septuagint is a collection of Greek translations of the Hebrew Bible often used by the writers of the New Testament.

up their biblical scrolls but were reprimanded by the Romans because the Romans, seeing how much the Jews revered these scrolls, were convinced that the Jews were carrying off *their sacred idols*, which the Romans likely believed offered special protection. That Luke imbues his eyewitness material with the same gravitas as these revered texts cannot be without significance—both Jews and Gentiles during this period knew that these texts were weighty and thus significant. What is particularly interesting is that this scriptural language clusters around the very places in Luke's text where he names key participants and where he also makes small, detailed changes from the written source(s) he is using. These changes are comparable, as we will see, to features in the memories of six Holocaust survivors who witnessed the final six months of Anne Frank's life.

Tell 4—Patterns of Convergence

A fourth tell we will explore could be called a "fractal tell": a convergence of features that collectively support the probability that an eyewitness source lay behind certain portions of Luke's text. These features include some we have already discussed: named persons, vivid details, and Semitic style. Other features, which we have yet to discuss, are also included: signs of primitivity and signs of inquiry, for example.

Tell 5—Patterns of Connectivity

The fifth tell builds from the fourth. There are areas in Luke's text where he consistently makes small changes or provides new information from his written source(s) in such a way that it creates a clear pattern of connection with, for instance, the Gospel of John. In this case, we will argue that this pattern is best explained by Luke's reliance on the Beloved Disciple as a living source.

Looking Ahead

Before looking at Luke's tells in detail throughout the following chapters, it is important to reemphasize the importance of tells and how these fit into a corroborative evidence case. Recall the difference between corroborative evidence versus mere cumulative evidence, as we discussed at the end of the Introduction. Corroborative evidence, while strengthening the main case, also strengthens one or several other pieces of evidence in the case simultaneously.

In this book we will argue, for example, that Luke's recall of personal names demonstrates his reliance on eyewitness sources; at the same time, this argument increases Luke's general reliability (i.e., it is also an argument for authenticity), which then in turns increases our confidence in Luke's claims to have relied on eyewitnesses (Luke 1:1–4). We will also discuss how Luke's vividness in recollecting his participation in a shipwreck demonstrates the likelihood that he was a traveling companion of Paul. On one level, this proves his proximity to eyewitness sources, but on another level it also proves Luke's interest in recalling detail accurately. This, then, adds weight to the argument that Luke likely had access to additional information whenever he adds additional, even varying, details to an account he borrows from Mark. When we notice that Luke tends to do this *in correspondence with the presence of a named person in the text*, it again strengthens our earlier argument about names in the text being indicate of eyewitness sources.

This is just one illustration of how this argument functions. Like an intertangled rope, some strands and strings are stronger than others. Some elements also function more like a tell than others do; that is, some patterns would be more difficult for Luke to craft intentionally than others.

The tells function as part of this corroborative case by supplying independence. Patterns only corroborate one another if they are independent, much like witnesses in a court of law. The strength of the tells in this regard should be clear. Because these patterns are, as we discussed, often extremely hard to mimic for someone not writing an authentic account but particularly difficult to avoid creating for someone who is, they provide the independent weight that we are looking for in a corroborative evidence case. The patterns are independent insofar that they are unintentional.[29]

Our study can only scratch the surface of what it might mean for the Gospel of Luke to contain eyewitness testimony. We will, for example, touch on issues such as memory variability, but we will not discuss the problem of miracles nor address the few well-known historical difficulties in Luke's text. These have been adequately discussed by other biblical scholars.[30] This study is meant to be fresh and positive, to infuse the ongoing discussion with some lines of evidence not previously explored. Although each Gospel will be treated at some length, the writings of Luke will certainly receive the greatest focus. This is because:

1. Focus has already been given to Matthew, Mark, and John in similar studies but not yet to the writings of Luke.

2. Renewed interests in Luke's claims as a historian and the unusual style of his Gospel allow for new insights into Luke's approach.

3. Luke's writings, as we will see, act as a hub, interconnecting various Gospel traditions.

4. Onomastic congruence, a feature to be defined shortly, is particularly pronounced in Luke-Acts, reflecting its historical interest and its proximity to eyewitness sources. This fea-

ture concerns patterns of names, which brings us to our next chapter and to our first tell.

TWO

Unintentional Byproduct

"What was your name again?" If you are like me, you have ut-
tered or thought this phrase before. If so, this is not the least
bit surprising. When it comes to our acquaintances, we tend to
forget their names very easily.[31] These names, for example, are
the most common types of words for TOT (tip-of-the-tongue)
experiences.[32] Furthermore, it is common to forget a person's
name while remembering their job but rare to forget their job
while remembering their name.[33] This tendency cannot be attributed to the relative infrequency or the particular form of a
name, since the occupation "baker" is consistently remembered
better than the name "Baker," a situation termed "the baker
paradox."[34] Memory is categorized around core ideas, and this
sheds light on why names are forgettable: they are generally arbitrary, difficult to image, and impossible to systematize in the
same way "baker" or "German" integrate into broader concepts.[35]
Names are often meaningless.

Even for unusually salient experiences, for which recall is most
vivid and enduring, names are the earliest casualties of memory
loss.[36] In ten vivid accounts of the 1944 massacre of Civitella,
wherein widows recall the execution of every male from their village, only few personal names are remembered.[37] A case in which
Holocaust survivors were questioned in 1984 and 1987 con-

cerning details also revealed in statements from 1943 and 1947 demonstrates that many details remained fixed over the forty-year span, while names were largely forgotten.[38] Travis Derico's investigations of oral traditions in northern Jordan reveal a unique exception: a case wherein many personal names are recalled over a long period of time—we return to this later.[39]

If memory is particularly frail in name recall—in other words, if names are meaningless, arbitrary, and difficult to image—why do certain ancient writings contain many authentic personal names? And this brings us to the Gospels. Can the study of names—a branch of scholarship called "onomastics"—be used as evidence to determine eyewitness sources behind ancient texts? Specifically, could this suggestion explain why the Gospels retain a significant amount of appropriately distributed names, even names that reflect their Aramaic pronunciations? (This is important because remember that Aramaic was likely the primary language spoken by Jesus' first followers.)

Answering in favor, Richard Bauckham observes that onomastics is seldom used and surprisingly little discussed in New Testament studies; the classicist Simon Hornblower calls it "deplorably underutilized" in studying ancient historical writings.[40] This portion of our study tips its hat towards this shortcoming, but it also results from initial misgivings about Bauckham's claims. Bauckham argues, in part, that the distribution of names in the Gospels—a feature we survey in-depth shortly—is an indication of authenticity because the relative frequencies of names in the Gospels reflect statistics within a database called the *Lexicon of Jewish Names in Late Antiquity: Part 1: Palestine 330 BCE—200 CE*. Because this database was put together by a Jewish scholar named Tal Ilan, I will refer to this database as "Ilan I" throughout this book.[41]

Because Ilan I is a key resource for our investigation, let me pause briefly to describe it. Ilan I is a prosopography. A prosopography is a modern resource, like a telephone book, which includes lists of names but also lists of persons bearing each name, often with relevant biographical details. The data that prosopographies catalogue, however, is ancient. Ilan I, for example, catalogues the names of 2953 fictional and nonfictional Jewish people named in sources from Palestine within the time span of 330 BCE to 200 CE. Ilan I is therefore used as a reference to determine the general naming patterns in the time/place of Jesus.[42]

One element of Bauckham's study especially invited my skepticism. Could an ancient author writing a fictional story not accomplish appropriate naming patterns if he (or she, although female authors were rare in antiquity) wanted to write something only *apparently* historical? For example, a New Testament scholar named Michael Strickland underappreciates how intricate the naming patterns in the Gospels are but succeeds in demonstrating that some appropriate names can be put into a work such as the *Protevangelium of James*, a later infancy gospel falsely attributed to the brother of Jesus.[43]

Responding to Bauckham's call to dig deeper into onomastics but also to an impulse to analyze his claims, I compiled my own list of named individuals from the Gospels and Acts as well as from twenty-three nonbiblical writings which, first, were comparable in length to the Gospels and Acts and, second, centered around one or two protagonists. Appendix A provides a full analysis of this research. This task created comparable data of approximately 1500 named persons from twenty-eight sources, including the five New Testament narratives alongside Greek romances, Greco-Roman biographies, and extrabiblical writings about Jesus and his followers.

Strengthening Bauckham's claims, my findings establish that appropriate and complex naming patterns like those found in several of the Gospels are characteristic of the most historically-oriented biographies from the Early Roman Empire (31 BCE–191 CE); further, the Gospels are also conservative in their treatment of names, and I discuss what this means and what it implies in the next chapter. As we will see, naming patterns are particularly telling in the writings of Luke, and this furthers the likelihood that this author named key informants in his texts.[44]

Onomastic Congruence

Onomastic congruence is a term I will use frequently; it refers to the creation of naming patterns by an ancient author that appropriately reflect the naming patterns of persons living in the time and place of a given narrative. The modern researcher observes onomastic congruence in the combination of three features in an ancient text: 1) A relatively significant number of appropriate proper names;[45] 2) a relatively increased level of detail in proper names; 3) patterns of proper names reflecting "the situation on the ground." These three features, as we will see, only come together in ancient literature that carries a significant historical interest (i.e., in historiographical works). Seldom will a non-historiographical work surveyed in our study contain any one of these three features; it never contains all three. This is suggestive. Although an unconscious act of the ancient author, onomastic congruence results from a conscious historiographical impulse at some level. It is not achieved otherwise. It is a tell of historicity.

Let me give some brief examples. The Infancy Gospel of Thomas is an extrabiblical gospel falsely attributed to the apostle Thomas (these are commonly called "apocryphal gospels"). It has eight names, for example, with "Thomas the Israelite" as the only

qualified name. In this case, "the Israelite" is an odd qualification for a person within an account where most other characters
are, likewise, Israelites. Aside from this unnatural qualification, a
Palestinian Jewish boy is named Zenon, a name quite common
in Delos and Athens but unusual for a Palestinian Jewish child.[46]
The Gospel of Nicodemus, another apocryphal gospel, has naming patterns that are completely incongruous: six of twenty-two
allegedly Jewish names are unattested in Ilan I[47] as are the names
of the two thieves crucified beside Jesus (Dismas and Gestas,
9.5); Ilan regards the former "without plausible explanation" and
the latter "obviously a literary invention."[48] Simply put, these
works do not hold up to scrutiny based on naming patterns, and
we can see the card player's bluff.

From my survey of twenty-three sources in Appendix A, the
only extra-biblical works that display onomastic congruence
are the works of Plutarch, Suetonius, and Josephus. Plutarch
(b. 46 CE) was a Greek biographer and perhaps the greatest of
antiquity; Suetonius (b. 69 CE), like Plutarch, is another well-
known historian and biographer of the Roman Caesars; Josephus, who lived approximately a generation after Jesus, was the
first Roman-Jewish historian. Josephus' *Life*—his autobiogra-
phy—has strong onomastic congruence. For example, out of
the ninety-three persons that Josephus names, six people are
named Simon, three people are named Matthias, four people are
named Jonathan, and six people are named Jesus. If we take this
random sampling of popular names in *Life*—Simon, Matthias,
Jonathan, and Jesus—these amount to 20.4% of named persons
in *Life* versus 16% in Ilan I. This is an example of onomastic
congruence—percentages of common names roughly match the
percentages of the same names in the relevant prosopography,
our ancient phonebook.[49]

The point is that out of the twenty-three extrabiblical writings I analyze in Appendix A, the biographies of Plutarch, Suetonius, and Josephus are the only ones that contain these sophisticated, corroborated naming patterns. These authors' works are the very same ones that the biblical scholar Craig Keener suggests mark the height of historical sensitivity for the genre of Greco-Roman biography when expectations of historical reliability were at their *highest*.[50] Onomastic congruence appears to be a byproduct, however unintentional, of the information-driven nature of these historiographical works. When the general aim of the ancient composition is historical, the author unintentionally checks all our boxes for onomastic congruence and whispers the truth of their hand. They cannot bluff this, as the extra-biblical gospels demonstrate, but neither can they hide this tell from the careful observer who is willing to take the time to investigate it.

THREE

Closer and Earlier

We finished our last chapter by noting that onomastic congruence appears to be a byproduct, however unintentional, of the
information-driven nature of certain biographies. But how about
the Gospels? How do they fair in terms of onomastic congruence?

Accurate naming patterns in the Gospels are demonstrated by
Richard Bauckham in *Jesus and the Eyewitnesses*. Bauckham first
refines Ilan I to exclude fictional names and then compares the
Gospels and Acts to the revised data. He highlights various examples of onomastic congruence. First, popular names are generally and appropriately qualified in the Gospels. This feature is also
well-demonstrated by Peter Williams, who provides the following illustration based on the list of the twelve apostles recorded in
the Gospel of Matthew (he adds in brackets the popular ranking
of names as determined by Bauckham):

> The names of the twelve apostles are these: first, Simon [1], who
> is called Peter, and Andrew [>99] his brother; James [11] the
> son of Zebedee, and John [5] his brother; Philip [61=] and Bar-
> tholomew [50=]; Thomas [>99] and Matthew [9] the tax col-
> lector; James [11] the son of Alphaeus, and Thaddaeus [39=];
> Simon [1] the Zealot, and Judas [4] Iscariot, who betrayed him.
> (Matthew 10.2–4)[51]

Williams adds the following comment:

> We see immediately that the more popular names, like Simon, Judas, Matthew, and James, have disambiguators, or, in the case of John, have clear contextual disambiguation (the name of his father). Disambiguators are used for the most popular eleven names. On the other hand, we have several names that, on Bauckham's rankings, are tied for thirty-ninth or lower in frequency: Thaddaeus, Bartholomew, Philip, and Thomas, which does not even make the top ninety-nine names. None of these have disambiguators. So not only are the names authentically Palestinian, but the disambiguation patterns are such as would be necessary *in Palestine, but not elsewhere* [emphasis his].[52]

Bauckham also highlights patterns of correspondence in the frequency of names. Simon and Joseph, the top two Jewish male names in the Gospels and Acts, for example, are also the top two in Ilan I (given to 18.2% of males in the NT narratives and to 15.6% of males in Ilan I). The names "Mary" or "Salome" apply to 38.9% of Jewish women in the Gospels and Acts; in Ilan I, the names apply to 28.6% of women. Increasing his scope, Bauckham observes that 41.5% of Jewish men in the general population, according to Ilan I, bear one of the nine most popular male names, whereas 40.3% do so in the Gospels and Acts.[53]

The most common names are always paired with details to make sure the reader knows who the writer is referring to (e.g., President Joe), while uncommon names are assumed to be specific enough (e.g., Obama). Common names also appear more frequently, like having three girls named Sarah in a third-grade class eight years after Sarah hit the number one spot on the baby names chart. Much like a poker player hiding a smile over an excellent hand, the Gospel authors cannot hide the accuracy of their historical observations.

Conservative Trends

Aside from onomastic congruence, the Synoptic Gospels also demonstrate several conservative trends in naming patterns.[†] Consider, for example, that Matthew and Luke never give a name to a person who is anonymous in the Gospel of Mark, although they sometimes drop names.[54] This could indicate conservatism when moving from early sources (Mark) to later (Matthew, Luke). Throughout our investigation, I assume that Mark was the first Gospel written and that Luke (and Matthew) used it as one of their sources. This position is widely held in biblical scholarship and almost taken for granted; I cite a helpful resource that summarizes the case in this book's endnotes.[55]

Ilan notes that New Testament authors uniquely transliterate Aramaic names, which leads to an almost entirely unique situation in the Gospels of the "Bar-" category of names (Bar meaning "son" in Aramaic): Barabbas, Barnabas, Bartimaeus, Barsabbas, Bar Jonah. In this list, Bar Jonah means "son of Jonah," for example, and Bartimaeus means "son of Timaeus." That the Gospels, especially Mark, retain these transliterations of Aramaic names reveals the Palestinian environment from which they come.[56] Other patterns reveal early *perspectives* as well. Mark, for example, consistently lists James son of Zebedee prior to his brother John (1.29; 3.16–19; 5.37; 9.2; 10.35; 13.3; 14.33). The account clearly considers James the more prominent disciple, even qualifying John son of Zebedee as "the brother of James" (1.29; 3.17; 5.37) despite John's rise to prominence after the death of James around 44 CE (cf. Gal. 2.9).

The relationship between Hebraic/Aramaic styles (i.e., Semitic styles) in the Greek text of the Gospels and onomastic data

---

[†] The Synoptic Gospels refer to Matthew, Mark, and Luke, who generally see things in a similar way, hence the term "Synoptic" which comes from the Greek word σύνοψις and carries that meaning of "seeing together."

is also significant, although this field of study is controversial.[57] Semitic style refers to syntax or vocabulary in the Gospels' Greek that reflects a Hebrew, Aramaic, or otherwise Jewish influence. A modern example would be what is commonly called "Dunglish," a form of English spoken, for example, by recent Dutch immigrants to America.

A Dutch immigrant might say, "What mean you?" instead of "What do you mean?" This is because the Dutch word order is reflected in the first form of the English question. Compound words in the Netherlands are very common, so Dunglish speakers will write creditcard, trainticket, and boardingpass as single words. These could also be called "Dutchisms," in the same way that the Greek Gospels sometimes have "Semitisms."

In a study of over seven hundred Semitisms in Luke, James Edwards concludes that material unique to Luke (L) contains four hundred percent more Semitisms than materials shared with Matthew/Mark.[58] Surprisingly, this highly Semitic material also contains twenty-eight of the forty-four named individuals in Luke. This amounts to 64% of named persons, although L only comprises 35% of the Gospel. Not only are named persons concentrated within more Semitic material, but less Semitic material also sees an increase of anonymous persons.[59] We will discuss what this means for Luke's Gospel in Chapter 6, but on the surface it indicates that names are conserved in Semitic materials while being less frequent in materials which are presumably later. "Presumably" must remain the operative word here. Scholars today are apt—contrary to Edwards—to attribute the Semitisms to Luke's own literary creativity rather than to his source materials. As we will discuss, this does not diminish the significance of the correlations.

To review and summarize, onomastic congruence increases as one looks closer and earlier into these texts. Our survey of onomastic data makes it apparent that the onomastic congruence of the Synoptic Gospels is comparative to the biographies of the Early Empire, and we are now prepared to consider what mechanism best explains onomastic conservatism in these cases.

FOUR

The Mechanism

So far, we have discussed onomastic congruence as an unintentional byproduct of authenticity. We saw that onomastic congruence in the Synoptic Gospels results from an especially conservative trend. But what best explains this phenomenon? It must be a mechanism that not only conserves information but also retains apparently meaningless information—names—in their original distributions and forms. Several factors suggest that this results from a mechanism that retained names of living informants or guarantors of the tradition.[60]

The first question facing the modern historian is why traditions ultimately stemming from Galilean peasants should contain complex and appropriate naming patterns in line with the compositions of Suetonius, Plutarch, and Josephus.[61] Plutarch and Suetonius were known to consult archival material. Suetonius utilized senate proceedings, wills, memoirs, and the imperial libraries, while Plutarch used fewer sources—memoirs, second-hand sources, eyewitness reports, letters, even oral traditions—but did so with more discretion.[62] Josephus, too, consulted witnesses, kept notes, and wrote from a perspective of informed familiarity.[63] Onomastic congruence is reflective of their archival repositories and historical interests. It is plausible that this likewise reflects, in the case of the Gospels, the archival repository available to them especially through living eyewitnesses. It readily explains the omission of minor characters' names from Mark's account by Matthew and Luke, the oral feature of many New Testament names (i.e., the "Bar-" category), and the concentration of names in primitive traditions versus the increased anonymity in non-Semitic materials. Again, the proposal that names were significant while they referred to living informants but were forgotten as these individuals died or became less prominent explains this data well. We cannot miss a further observation. The Evangelists, like other biographers in the ancient world, were unafraid to creatively shape their accounts, as we discuss in Chapters 10–12. Whether with or without design, the Gospel authors accumulated differences, altered details, and created theological color, but they did not add names.[64] The issue of Gospel differences can be prickly, and when I say that they contain differences, I do not mean that these differences cannot be reconciled; maybe they cannot be, or maybe they can. My point here is simply about names: these were treated with a *special* conservatism.

Names also cluster around significant functions and events. Lists of the Twelve (Mark 3.16–19; Matt. 10.2–4; Luke 6.14–16; Acts 1.13), unlike comparable Rabbinic lists (*m. 'Abot* 2.8–14; *b. Sanh. 43a*), appear to function for the sheer purpose of conserving the names of authoritative eyewitnesses.[65] While their individual significance is eventually eclipsed by their mere "twelveness," suggesting a fading role, the lists show independence and several signs of primitivity: again, the prominence of James son of Zebedee over John (Mark 3.17; Matt. 10.2; Luke 6.14), Aramaisms (Βοανηργές, Βαρθολομαῖος), appropriate qualifiers, and mnemonic features to aid in memory.[66]

The named women at the tomb are particularly significant. Carolyn Osiek argues for the primitivity of these narratives and that a general male bias rather than legal considerations (cf. Josephus, *Ant.* 4.219) caused the omission of their accounts until their "explosion" into public proclamation through the Gospels.[67] The retention of specific and even variant lists of names may suggest that these women continued to function individually as witnesses of their experiences during intervening years—a situation strengthened by the consideration that "Joanna, the wife of Chuza, Herod's steward," present at the tomb and also in Luke 8.2–3, would have, along with Manaen (Acts 13.1), been a valuable informant for Luke's unique material on Herod Antipas. Beyond this, there is an incidental connection to the Gospel of Matthew at this point. Matthew 14.1–2 reads: "He [Herod] said to his attendants, 'This is John the Baptist; he has risen from the dead! That is why miraculous powers are at work in him.'" One is left to wonder how Matthew could glean this information about a comment Herod appears to have made in private to his servants, but Luke provides the answer in his earlier description of Joanna as "wife of Chuza, the *steward* of Herod's household" (Luke 8.3).[68] Joanna and her husband could have been sources for the Gospel writers, including Luke.

Some named individuals or sets of individuals were already incorporated into creedal statements shortly after Jesus' death (e.g., Peter, James, and the Twelve; cf. 1 Cor. 15.3–8). That the Gospel of Mark, possibly a performed text, especially retained certain names (Jairus, Bartimaeus, Simon of Cyrene and his sons) suggests the possibility of their significance in early oral performances within certain communities.[69] Third, Kenneth Bailey and Travis Derico have observed the presence of specially designated storytellers/eyewitnesses in modern oral-based villages in the Middle East. As noted at the beginning of Chapter 2, Derico's transcripts of interviews from his fieldwork in Jordan reveal an unusually high concentration of names. Although elements of Bailey's theory have been thoroughly critiqued by Theodore Weeden, Bailey's claim that personal names were conserved during the transmission of what he calls "informal, controlled oral tradition" remains unchallenged.[70] Rainer Riesner's observations also consider the unique *religious* context of Jesus' ministry, a context amenable to a high retention of sacred tradition; Riesner notes that Jesus taught in memorable form, preached regularly in the synagogue, prompted radical devotion, and specifically established tradents (i.e., persons designated to pass down oral tradition) to carry on his teachings.[71] Names of these individuals and other informants were especially conserved as living footnotes of the oral repository, explaining why a pattern of onomastic congruence on par with the most historically robust biographies of antiquity should be found in the communal memories of an itinerant Galilean rabbi.

The very occurrence of onomastic congruence in the Synoptic Gospels, therefore, with names uniquely conserved and clustering around significant functions and events, suggests the footnoting of living eyewitness sources, and we can draw parallels from ancient historiographical sources for this even among those historians in the Thucydidean tradition who, like Luke, subtly concealed their sources within their narratives.[72] Onomastic congruence in Luke-Acts, indeed, beyond tying Luke to the "oral archive" of early eyewitnesses also reflects its broader historiographical interest. Luke-Acts contains 127 personal names in total, reflecting contemporary historiographical works in terms of name-density, and Luke's writings bear strong onomastic congruence across various spectrums. Let us look at one example to close off this chapter.

Patterns

The importance of this first tell relies on a complex pattern of evidence, and a lack of appreciation for such a pattern can cloud our judgements. David Gill's analysis of the name Damaris in

Acts 17.34, for example, is a good illustration of an unsound conclusion in this regard.[73] He argues that Damaris is likely a name invented by Luke partly because it is a singly attested Greek name.[74] Several errors undermine this reasoning. First, the philologist Sterling Dow observes that one in twenty-five ancient Greek names is unique; Acts 16–28 contains nineteen Greek names, two of which are unique (Damaris, 17.14; Lydia, 16.14), conforming to the general pattern.[75] Interestingly, Apollos, mentioned in Acts 18.24, is also rarely attested in the relevant Greek prosopographies because it is not a Greek name; it is Egyptian (attested widely in Alexandria), where Apollos, according to the author of Acts, is said to originate. Gill's error is worsened by actual statistics now provided in more recently published databases, which place rarity of Greek names in Coastal Asia at nine to ten percent rather than Dow's four percent, making Acts resemble the onomastic situation on the ground even more precisely.[76] Acts 17.34 also contains another name—Dionysius—one of the most popular names. Dionysius is qualified ("member of the Areopagus") while Damaris, a rare name, is not.[77]

Acts 16–20 also contains three names that are theophoric (i.e., names that incorporate the name(s) of God/gods): Timothy (Τιμόθεος, 16.1), Demetrius (Δημήτριος, 19.24), and Dionysius (Διονύσιος, 17.34). This makes three out of nineteen (15.8 percent) theophoric, also resembling a typical onomastic situation along the ancient northern Mediterranean according to a recently published database.[78] Once again, Luke unintentionally gives careful readers another clue to his historical care. Such fidelity extends to Luke's treatment of names on the lips of characters. For example, Luke consistently writes Simon Peter's given name in its Hellenized form throughout his Gospel (i.e., as Σίμων: Luke 4.38; 5.3; 5.4; 5.5; 5.8; 5.10; 6.14; 22.31), yet in Acts 15.14

he appropriately switches to the Semitic form of Simon's name, Συμεών, when placing it on the lips of Jesus' brother, James. (Is this a sign of Luke's personal awareness of how James referred to Peter in this instance?) That such an astonishing level of onomastic congruence exists within the last half of Acts, with the majority of these names occurring in the few brief "we" sections (to be discussed shortly), also concurs well with the traditional portrait of Luke as Paul's traveling companion. It is to this issue that we turn next.

FIVE

Intention [79]

Acts 27.1–28.15, the tail end of Luke's sequel to his Gospel, provides the most vivid, lengthy account in Acts (six percent of its overall length).[80] The German New Testament scholar Marius Reiser, in drawing a comparison with accounts from other ancient writers like Lucian (*Nav.* 7–9), Plutarch (*Dio.* 25.1–11), and Aelius Aristides (*H.S.*, 4.32–36), goes further and calls it the most thorough and historically accurate shipwreck account in ancient history.[81] As part of a "we" section (sections of Acts wherein the author writes as if he is present alongside others by using the first-person plural), it is often the subject of creative speculation concerning its origin, aim, and genre. There are two features that support its reading as eyewitness recollection.

First, it bears the marks of what the scholar Colin Hemer compares to the rough texture of newly deposited stones on a beach.[82] Rather than the smooth, tempered details Luke gives in other sections of Acts, this account bears features that seem comparatively unrefined (e.g., superfluous and unusual nautical terms, extensive references of hope for survival, names of insignificant islands and ports, etc.); indeed, Luke mentions sixteen place names in Acts 27.1–28.15 from a total of eight-five in Acts (i.e., although six percent of its length, it contains over eighteen percent of its place names).[83] John Gilchrist likens these features to those of a specimen as it is viewed under the microscope—the overall shape of the item lost in the minutia of detail.[84] Although vivid, personal, and historically pertinent details permeate the account, its comparable significance for the overarching narrative is far from obvious; Gilchrist, indeed, regards the account—along with the other "we" sections—as a seeming parody of the book of Acts itself.[85]

Second, some details are so striking as to discourage any reading other than eyewitness recollection. These include:

- The accurate sailing times compared to the distances of ports, direction of sailing, and the relevant meteorological factors.[86]
- The correct naming of ports and villages, even minor and irrelevant to the narrative but confirmed by early documentary sources in local dialect—sometimes despite incorrect locations in extant geographical works (e.g., the location of the island named Καῦδα, cf. Ptolemy and Pliny).[87]
- Nautical jargon, such as εὐρακύλων (27.14) and σκάφη (27.16), now confirmed as likely Greek transliterations of Latin descriptive terms.[88]
- The presence of superfluous accurate detail, even concerning sailing maneuvers of which the writer himself seems aloof.[89]

These details form a cohesive historical picture. This ship would be pledged to the emperor, therefore amenable and subject to a centurion (Acts 27.11, 43) but privately owned and operated by Roman sailors.[90] A fourteen-day journey with a heavy northeastern wind driving a sizable ship on the starboard tack would take them the 476.6 miles from Cauda to Point Koura on the trajectory described by Luke.[91] The presence of like detail alone in Pliny the Elder's account of gold mining in Spain is enough to conclude the presence of eyewitness testimony, although Pliny's account completely lacks any literary first person indicators like those present in Acts 27.1–28.15.[92]

What explains the vividness of this account, its uncanny accuracy, its disproportionate length, and its emotional color? Why should patterns of vividness in Acts concentrate within the "we" narratives and especially within the narrative realism and local detail of Acts 27.1–28.15? In my 2019 *Tyndale Bulletin* article, "Acts 27–28: The Cerebral Scars of Shipwreck," I argued that it was likely the traumatic nature of surviving the shipwreck that led Luke to recount its journey with such detail and accuracy. I now believe there is more to it than that.

As we see shortly in Chapters 7 and 8, even the most salient firsthand experience will not naturally be remembered with scientific accuracy. This is simply not how memory works. Several thousand published studies now weigh into the discussion of eyewitness memories.[93] Variables undermining true recollection include: weapon focus, high-stress environment, inadequate duration of experience, poor lighting, far distance, memory decay, unconscious transference, adolescence or old age, intoxication, and cross-racial identification.[94] Additional studies highlight the potential for memory manipulation through police procedure, subsequent reporting, and personal influences that distort and/ or create false memories.[95] Our discussion in Chapter 2 revealed that some details, especially personal names, are most prone to such distortion and forgetfulness.

Even findings that confirm the potential reliability of memory do not explain the extremely high accuracy of Luke's "we" narratives, esp. Acts 27.1–28.15. Robert McIver relates an interesting incident in British Columbia wherein thirteen eyewitnesses to a violent crime were questioned concerning a range of seventeen to ninety-five details. The average accuracy during the initial police interviews was eighty-two percent but dropped by only one percent over a period of three months. Significantly, false information distributed through media outlets did not impact accuracy of recollection, nor did several misleading questions create false memories.[96] That is good recall, but *not* as good as Luke's recall. As we see in Chapters 7 and 8, the details in Luke's account that we can corroborate—the accurate timings of sailings, the renderings of names in appropriate dialect—are the very types of details most prone to variation and/or distortion.

A better explanation is that Luke took measures to ensure that he would remember well. Perhaps he took notes of the journeys. Perhaps he was intentional in making observations. This intention to recount events with accuracy appears to have progressed throughout his various travels with Paul, especially after Paul's two-year imprisonment in Caesarea, near Jerusalem, just prior to the journey that led to his shipwreck. This pattern of vividness/accuracy in the "we" sections is a tell that establishes not only Luke's eyewitness participation in certain travels of Paul, but it also increases the likelihood that Luke interviewed living informants in the making of Luke-Acts as part of his own increasing awareness as a chronicler of the Jesus movement. Five observations strengthen this possibility:

- In the late 50s CE—during Luke's alleged presence with Paul—the total number of Christians was still modest; Rodney Stark estimates the number at approximately 2000.[97]

- Churches at this time were still limited almost entirely to independent house churches, where intimate contact with early disciples would have been achievable.[98]

- Many eyewitnesses to Jesus' private and public ministry would still be alive (Robert McIver arrives at a number of approximately fifteen thousand by the year 60 CE, based upon population statistics, sizes of crowds, and projected lifespans).[99] Some of these individuals are named as Paul's acquaintances (i.e., possibly Andonicus and Junia, Rom. 16.7; Peter, John, and James, Gal. 2.9; again, James, Acts 15.13; James and "all the elders," Acts 21.18; possibly Mnason, Acts 21.16).

- The "we" narratives place Luke in the vicinity of Jerusalem for approximately two years (Acts 24.27, 57–59 CE).

- At this time Christians were a tight-knit group of prolific networkers, as extant sources demonstrate.[100]

If we follow the "we" sections carefully, we notice several names of likely informants *en route*. The author mentions, incidentally, the name of a minor character, Mnason from Cyprus (Acts 21.16), whose house he lodged in on the way to Jerusalem, mentioning him as an "early" (ἀρχαῖος, original/ancient) disciple. Likewise, the author mentions lodging with Philip the Evangelist, another potential source for several detailed accounts (Acts 6; 8.26–39; 21.8–9).[101] If the author of Luke-Acts intends to emulate the Thucydidean craft already by this time, these would not be mere chance encounters but would exemplify the ancient historian's commitment to travel; in such a scenario, the most significant destination in the "we" narratives is certainly Palestine, where Luke in 57–59 CE could have gleaned the information which is now associated with Luke's special traditions embodying "the perspectives of some of the same recurring persons, notably Mary, Peter, James and John, beside such as Martha, Zacchaeus and Cleopas in isolated instances."[102] As we will observe more closely under our next tell, these same names specifically coincide with areas in Luke's Gospel that contain concentrations of Semitisms.

SIX

To Tell It Like the Scriptures

Ik hou van jou. You likely do not understand the words I just typed, but my wife surely does. The words are written in Dutch, and this might make you conclude that my wife is from the Netherlands. You would be mistaken. My wife is one hundred percent American, while I am the Dutch immigrant. *Ik hou van jou* is a phrase she wanted me to teach her—it means "I love you," but, according to her, it sounds more romantic when I say it in Dutch.

Communicators often switch the register of their language, or even switch to another language altogether, to highlight something important or to make an important connection with their audience. Scholars sometimes call this "code-switching." President Trump tweets in all-capital letters. President Obama turns to a waitress in a diner in Washington, D.C. and, responding to her question about whether he wants to keep the change, says, "Nah, we straight." Preachers might pray or even preach in sentences of King James English. Scholars might switch, without warning, to quoting texts in their relevant research languages.

Although we referenced James Edwards' observations about the Semitic flavor of certain portions of Luke's Gospel (see Chapter 3), the most comprehensive work to date on the topic is a technical treatise titled *Semitisms in Luke's Greek: A Descriptive Analysis of Lexical and Syntactical Domains of Semitic Language*

Influence in Luke's Gospel by Albert Hogeterp and Adelbert De-naux.[103] This book contains extensive engagement with primary and secondary sources, comparative analyses, and critical evaluation of all possible Semitisms in Luke's Gospel in terms of vocabulary and syntax. It earns, in my opinion, Craig Blomberg's evaluation that this work is "invaluable, and it is hard to imagine the work being superseded at any point in the near future."[104]

Its two authors determine a complex set of backgrounds for Luke's Semitisms, including influence from the LXX, biblical Hebraic, Aramaic, and possible Syro-Palestinian bilingualism. Their conclusion is that Luke's Semitic flavor could come from a variety of places—possibly from his source materials, possibly from his own knowledge of Semitic traditions, but most frequently from his own proclivity to write in a style that his audience would be accustomed to seeing or hearing in their sacred Scriptures. *That is, Luke varies the Semitic flavor of his narrative intentionally, infusing appropriate accounts with Semitisms and rich biblical allusions in line with the rhetorical aims of his prologue: to convey a sense of reliability* (ἀσφάλειαν, 1.4).[105]

There has been some debate over Luke's usage of καθεξῆς σοι γράψαι in Luke 1.4, usually translated something like, "to write an orderly account for you [that is, for Theophilus]." An analysis of the term καθεξῆς as used in Luke-Acts does not indicate that it refers to a strictly chronological ordering of material.[106] The NIV translates καθεξῆς in Acts 11.4, for example, in terms of "telling the whole story." It suggests putting events in their appropriate perspective. Luke, then, has placed the events of his Gospel into proper perspective for Theophilus. One way he does this is by using biblical language to frame various accounts in his biography of Jesus.

Three recurring Semitisms are especially prominent as discourse markers—that is, as key words that make up the narrative introductions which frame the smaller units of Luke's Gospel:

- (καί) ἐγένετο (δέ), mirroring biblical Hebrew: וַיְהִי (and it happened/came about)
- ἐν τῷ + infinitive (literally, "in the to + verbal noun," mirroring a Hebrew idiom)
- καί ἰδού[107] ("and behold," a common Semitism in the LXX)

Figure 1 below is based on Appendix B in the back, which catalogues all Semitisms unique to Luke (as compared to Matthew and Mark) as determined by Hogeterp and Denaux.[108] As Figure 1 demonstrates, heavy concentrations of Semitisms and especially Lukan discourse markers concentrate, often in introductions, around accounts that focus on eyewitnesses, many of whom are named in the narratives.[109] Thus, our code-switching approach to Semitisms is different from seeing the Semitisms as indicators of earlier, Semitic sources. Yet it still aligns with Edwards' observations, as discussed in Chapter 3, that clusters of Semitisms coincide with named individuals in Luke.

FIGURE 1		
Location	**Nature of Content**	**Semitisms**
5.1–2a	Extra material on the call of Peter and the first disciples	Periphrastic imperfect
		Unstressed καὶ αὐτός
		ἐν τῷ+ infinitive
		Parataxis
		(καὶ) ἐγένετο (δέ)
5.12	Extra material on healing of man with leprosy	(καὶ) ἐγένετο (δέ)
		ἐν τῷ+ infinitive
		καὶ ἰδού
		Parataxis
		Lack of the copula εἰμί

5.17	Extra material on healing of paralytic	Periphrastic imperfect (καὶ) ἐγένετο (δέ) Unstressed καὶ αυτός Parataxis
5.18		ἄνθρωπος ἐνώπιον w/gen.
7.11	Special material on widow in Nain	(καὶ) ἐγένετο (δέ)
7.12		καὶ ἰδού Parataxis
8.1	Special material with list of women who served Jesus and the Twelve	Unstressed καὶ αυτός (καὶ) ἐγένετο (δέ) Parataxis
9.28	Extra Petrine material on Jesus' transfiguration	(καὶ) ἐγένετο (δέ) After these things (bib)
9.29		(καὶ) ἐγένετο (δέ) ἐν τῷ+ infinitive
9.33		(καὶ) ἐγένετο (δέ) ἐν τῷ+ infinitive
9.34		ἐν τῷ+ infinitive
9.36		In those days ἐν τῷ+ infinitive
9.37		(καὶ) ἐγένετο (δέ)
9.38		ἀνήρ καὶ ἰδού
9.39		καὶ ἰδού

9.51	Key verse on Jesus setting his face to Jerusalem	ἐν τῷ + infinitive (καὶ) ἐγένετο (δέ) Unstressed καὶ αυτός πρόσωπον (bib) ἀποστέλλειν πρὸ προσώπου with genitive
9.53		πρόσωπον Periphrastic imperfect
11.27	Special comment from a woman in the crowd	(καὶ) ἐγένετο (δέ) ἐν τῷ + infinitive
13.11	Special material on healing of a crippled woman	καὶ ἰδού Lack of copula εἰμί
13.14		ἀποκριθεὶς/εἶσα εἶπεν ἐρχόμενος/ἐλθών
13.16		σατανᾶς ἰδού as particle for time
14.1	Special material about Jesus in the house of a prominent Pharisee	(καὶ) ἐγένετο (δέ) ἐν τῷ + infinitive Periphrastic imperfect Parataxis
14.2		καὶ ἰδού
14.3		ἀποκριθεὶς/εἶσα εἶπεν
17.11	Jesus heals men with leprosy	(καὶ) ἐγένετο (δέ) ἐν τῷ + infinitive Parataxis
17.13		Unstressed καὶ αυτός
17.14		(καὶ) ἐγένετο (δέ) πορευθείς/έντες

17.17		ἀποκριθεὶς/εῖσα εἶπεν
17.19		ἀναστάς/ᾶσα/άντες with verb of movement
17.21		Lack of the copula εἰμί
18.35	Extra material on Bartimaeus (in Jericho)	(καὶ) ἐγένετο (δέ) ἐν τῷ+ infinitive
19.2	Special material on Zacchaeus (in Jericho)	καὶ ἰδού Unstressed καὶ αυτός (twice) Lack of the copula εἰμί
19.11	Parable given before Zacchaeus and crowd in Jericho	(καὶ) ἐγένετο (δέ)
19.15		(καὶ) ἐγένετο (δέ) ἐν τῷ+ infinitive Parataxis (καὶ) ἐγένετο (δέ)
22.31	Extra Petrine material	τοῦ + infinitive σατανᾶς
24.4	Women at the tomb	(καὶ) ἐγένετο (δέ) ἐν τῷ+ infinitive Parataxis
24.13	Cleopas/road to Emmaus	καὶ ἰδού Periphrastic imperfect
24.14		Unstressed καὶ αυτός
24.15		(καὶ) ἐγένετο (δέ) ἐν τῷ+ infinitive
24.17		Lack of the copula εἰμί
24.18		ἀποκριθεὶς/εῖσα εἶπεν

I have not translated all the material in Figure 1 because I will translate the relevant portions when discussing them in following chapters. Some of the Semitic clusters align with the theological aims of Luke (e.g., 9.28, 9.51) as he arranges his material concerning the τῶν πεπληροφορημένων ἐν ἡμῖν πραγμάτων ("the things that have been *fulfilled* among us," Luke 1.1).[110] In this case Luke may be stylizing his text to highlight a biblically significant event.[111]

Related to this phenomenon may be the practice of ancient historians to tag their source information with various indicators.[112] Some material, such as the transfiguration details surrounding Peter, may be tagged by Luke for both their historical and theological value; these need not be mutually exclusive.[113] Plutarch, as an illustration, could highlight the eyewitness presence of Asinius Pollio to legitimize a key anecdote in his literary portrait of Caesar: Caesar's crossing of the Rubicon (*Caes.* 32.3–6).[114] Luke, likewise, could accentuate the historicity of situations for the very reason that he also finds them theologically significant and vice versa.

As an example, we could take the first two chapters of Luke's Gospel, commonly called "Luke's Infancy Narrative," a text replete with Semitisms.† This material comes to focus on Mary the mother of Jesus, an issue we revisit in Chapter 11. The account is also adorned with allusions to Genesis, Exodus, 1 and 2 Samuel, Daniel, Isaiah, and the Psalms. Further, it is written in the style of these texts. From the outset, Theophilus would see the Scriptures of the ancient past continuing and being fulfilled as he begins to read Luke's Gospel. Yet the narrative is about an unremarkable virgin and her promised son. The account of this girl, however, is placed in biblical proportion by Luke. Theophi-

---

†I excluded the Semitisms of this section from Figure 1 because of the sheer volume of Semitisms therein. The total amounts to forty-six according to Hogeterp and Denaux's calculations, which is fifteen percent of total unique Semitisms in Luke's Gospel.

lus would have been left with an impression that likely mirrored Luke's own conviction. Mary's experience, as recounted in the Infancy Narrative, is not just a story. It is history. It is God's revelation. It is no less than Scripture.

It is further possible, of course, that the Infancy Narrative and his account of the transfiguration were biblically significant for Luke because they were biblically significant for Mary and Peter, respectively. In other words, it is possible that the eyewitnesses *themselves* inspired the biblical interpretations of their own experiences. This could explain a few features of Luke's text.

In the "we" passages of Acts and the prologue to his Gospel, Luke is least likely to be dependent on sources. Likewise, there are very few Semitisms in these sections, if any. A prologue in antiquity was like a modern "table of contents," and since Luke evidently saw much of his project as a continuity of the Hebrew Scripture, why did he not adorn his own prologue with Semitisms?[115] Why not recount his travels with Paul in a biblical flavor? It is likely that Luke did not deem his own perspective worthy of being counted on par with Scripture. His prologue and travels are, first and foremost, those of a historian and not a theologian.[116]

That the "scripturalizing" of Luke's text may have been influenced by the eyewitnesses also explains the various biblical portraits of Jesus within his Gospel. His narrative does not convey a singular perspective of Jesus, as we will see in Chapters 10–12.[117] Some portions of his Gospel focus on Jesus' Davidic, regal aspects; some texts highlight Jesus' prophetic ministry. Even within Jesus' prophetic role, some passages in Luke's Gospel tie him to Elijah/Elisha, while others tie him to the Suffering Servant of Isaiah or to Moses. This is what one would expect if Luke conserved various interpretations of Jesus' ministry. These different portraits of Jesus, like the Semitisms in his Gospel, concentrate in sections that tie back to primitive traditions (see Chapter 10) or specific persons such as Mary or Peter (see Chapters 11–12).

Luke himself seems to suggest that his living sources were also authoritative exegetes—i.e., that the eyewitnesses and biblical interpreters were one and the same. Luke calls these sources "eyewitnesses *and* servants of the word" (Luke 1.2).[118] He could have perceived these "servants" akin to the synagogue "servant" (see Luke 4.20) placed in charge of guarding and distributing the biblical scrolls.[119] The eyewitnesses, likewise, were those whose eyes had been specifically opened to understand the Scriptures (Luke 24.25, 27, 32, 44, and 45). When Jesus revealed himself to Cleopas and his companion on the road to Emmaus, for example, Luke underscores this point by using the same verb (διανοίγω) to describe their understanding of the Scriptures and the opening of their eyes (Luke 24.31, 32).[120] They were eyewitnesses to more than Jesus' life. Their eyes had been opened to see this life in its biblical perspective.

I am *not* saying that Luke never creatively adapted a received tradition. I *am* saying what we suggested at the end of our Introduction: Luke's use of eyewitness testimony and his literary creativity can be seen as complementary as opposed to contradictory. The historical tells noted so far—Luke's achievement of onomastic congruence, his increased vividness when he himself is an eyewitness in the "we" passages of Acts, and the alignment of names with Semitic structural markers—form a portrait of Luke as an author with an interest in eyewitness accounts.

But can we learn anything more from the texts that Luke has, so to speak, written in sacred tongue or whispered to us in our native language? Texts that Luke has strategically scripturalized? A unique situation now allows us to go deeper by looking at patterns of variation.

Often a named person and a Semitic cluster will coincide with portions of Luke's text wherein he deviates from Mark's account. One example in Luke's Gospel concerns Joanna. Luke introduces the two accounts in which he names her with Semitic discourse markers (Luke 8.1, Luke 24.1). Remember that Luke also highlights her relationship with Chuza, the steward of Herod Antipas. One further area of interest, then, is Luke's unique insight into Herod Antipas (Luke 9.9; 8.31–3; 23.8–12) and his willingness to vary from Mark concerning comments about Herod (Mark 6.14–16 vs. Luke 9.9; Mark 6.17 vs. Luke 3.19). We will survey these types of variations over the next two chapters. First, we will see that they occur between independent personal event memories of Holocaust survivors as well. Second, we will see that they occur in *similar types of detail* between the Gospels of Luke and Mark. But where in Luke's Gospel do these variations occur? In the very portions of Luke's Gospel that center around named individuals and include Luke's scriptural tags.

SEVEN

After the Achterhuis

Anne Frank's diary penned from 1940 to 1942 from *Het Achterhuis* (lit. "the backhouse," typically translated as "the secret annex") of her father's office in downtown Amsterdam is now among the most read books in history, being published in over fifty countries.[121] An often-quoted journal entry from July 15, 1944 reads: "Toch houd ik ze vast, ondanks alles, omdat ik nog steeds aan de innerlijke goedheid van den mens geloof" ("I still hold fast [to my ideals], because in spite of everything, I still believe in the innate goodness of humanity").[122] Several weeks after this entry, on August 4, the Franks were taken to Westerbork in Drente, and the events that follow—according to the interviews of six Dutch women in the 1980s—cast doubt on the idyllic perspective with which Anne's diary closes.

These six women, Hannah Elisabeth Pick-Goslar (HP), Janny Brandes-Brilleslijper (JB), Rachel van Amerongen-Frankfoorder (RF), Bloeme Evers-Emden (BE), Lenie de John-van Naarden (LJ), and Ronnie Goldstein-van Cleef (RG), were witnesses through various points of the final seven months of Anne Frank's life. Their testimonies are supplemented by oral histories from Helen Waterford (HW) and Anne Frank's stepsister, Eva Schloss (ES).[123] These women passed through the transport station of Westerbork in Drente, rode in cattle cars to Auschwitz-Birkenau, and some lodged with Anne Frank in Bergen-Belsen, where she died of typhus sometime in February 1945. Further, these women endured the same sufferings and surreal experiences many Holocaust survivors feel morally bound to memorialize. Several women were initially reluctant to share their stories with Mr. Lindwer, who spent over two years building the necessary rapport to capture his interviews with them in Dutch.[124] These were later translated into English and published in 1991 under the title: *The Last Seven Months of Anne Frank*. Several features of *The Last Seven Months* commend them as adequate candidates for a comparison with possible eyewitness-based texts in the Gospel of Luke:

- These interviews contain recollections from a comparative time lapse (forty years).
- They contain memories of events perhaps only accessible through personal testimony.
- They have passed through a single layer of translation (Dutch to English).
- They center around a set of local events in time and place.
- They are ideologically driven and interested in shaping an impression.[125]

A few objections could be given against the analogy. The first would press for a greater expectation of reliability for testimony recorded in the Gospels—were not the memory capacities of ancients, after all, more exercised and therefore more robust than those of modern people? The second objection would push in favor of a greater expectation of the Gospels' unreliability—were the eyewitnesses behind the Gospels not evangelists in the popular sense, and therefore prone to recite, repeat, and distort their recollections, especially compared to the reluctant survivors of the Holocaust?

The situation is complex. Specialists in memory studies differentiate between the memories of literate and illiterate people, for example, with the latter being seen as more prone to recalling the mere gist or theme and not the exact wording of information.[126] It is possible, of course, that some of Jesus' disciples were literate; more so, it is likely that other factors, such as Jesus' role as a religious teacher propagating a message and apprenticing pupils, would increase the tendencies for more reliable memory.[127] Collective memories, likewise, would play a controlling role, but it is not unlikely that such a role, likewise, influenced the memories of Holocaust survivors. Eva Schloss, stepdaughter of Otto Frank, spoke frequently about her experiences during the Holocaust and, indeed, was part of a movement to ensure the preservation of the memories of Holocaust survivors for future generations. Even if certain witnesses to these events did not speak of their experiences initially, their fellow survivors, their personal identities, and their shared society would have played an overwhelming role in the preservation of their memories. This cannot be entirely different from the experiences following Easter morning for the early witnesses of Jesus' ministry.

The claim is not that the analogy between these Holocaust survivors and the potential eyewitness sources behind Luke's Gospel is the only analogy we should seek to draw. The claim is neither that the analogy is flawless. Instead, the assertion is that an appreciation for the types of variability that occur in the Anne Frank narratives gives us yet another set of data by which to compare the differences that Luke creates in his changes of Mark's text. I will weigh the explanatory power of this analogy at the end of our analysis.

First, I will analyze these accounts from Anne Frank's final months and note some points of difference and similarity. In the next chapter, I will analyze similar patterns in accounts from Luke's Gospel.

After the *Achterhuis*: An Analysis

Anne Frank, her sister Margot, and her parents are betrayed, along with others in the *achterhuis*, and are taken from their hiding place at No. 263 Prinsengracht on August 4, 1944. They travel first to Westerbork, a transfer station in the Netherlands, where they stay until September 3, 1944. On the final transport out, cattle cars take them and over one thousand others to Auschwitz/Birkenau; only 127 survive.[128] Anne's mother perishes there shortly after Anne and Margot are moved again to Bergen-Belsen, where both girls likely succumb to typhus shortly before liberation. Anne's father, Otto Frank, survives, returning to the *achterhuis* in the summer of 1945, where Miep Gies, his secretary, gives him Anne's diary. Otto devotes the rest of his life to promoting the diary, raising awareness of the Holocaust and honoring her memory.

Considerable discrepancies exist when comparing Lindmer's 1988 interviews of the six female witnesses. For the sake of brevity, I include only recollections of the Franks' journey and stay in Auschwitz/Birkenau in the text below, but these samples should suffice to demonstrate the level and type of variations typical of personal event memories recalled forty years after such an experience.

Trip to Auschwitz

The trip from the transfer station at Westerbork to Auschwitz on September 3, 1944, is unanimously remembered as extremely unpleasant; various details, however, either confirm or contradict one another. Significantly, JB remembers the belligerence of people aboard, while LJ recounts their respect for one another and that men, for example, allowed the elderly to sit; BE says that there was no room to sit or sleep. RF remembers that people had to relieve themselves where they stood, while LJ remembers a pail, although she mentions that it filled up quickly and had to be drained through a crack in the cattle car. No one agrees on the length of the journey: four days (JB), countless hours (BE), two days and nights (LJ). RG says the doors were nailed shut while LJ remarks they were bolted. They all agree that the journey was long and difficult and that they rode in cattle cars; LJ estimated seventy people per car, while an independent witness (HW) remarked there were one hundred to one hundred-twenty. Several women remember a tall gentleman who peered through a small, high window and relayed details of the journey (RF, LJ), while RF remembers that he was a Pole named Leo. Both recall that it was him who first relayed the news that their destination would be Auschwitz.

Arrival in Auschwitz

Only JB recalls the gate at Auschwitz and the sign, ARBEIT MACHT FREI ("work sets you free"). JB and LJ recall the loudspeaker, while most women comment on seeing prisoners in striped outfits (BE, LJ, RG) and oppressive lights which are described as neon and bluish (JB), bright (HW), very powerful (BE), and yellow (RG). LJ cannot remember if it was morning or evening, while JB says the sky was gray, and RG recalls that it was night. After their arrival, most remember that all baggage had to be left in the cars, although BE remembers taking in her baggage. After this, there was a separation of women from men (LJ), after which the very old/young were selected immediately for the crematorium. RG remembers Mengele saying, "This side, that side!", while HP recounts him saying, in German, "Rechts, links!" There is agreement that all women were stripped completely naked (except for shoes, LJ), tattooed, "showered" (with a trickle of water), and thrown a bundle of clothes (LJ), or only a dress (HW).

Birkenau

After arriving in Auschwitz, the women were marched to Birkenau—a women's camp that formerly sheltered the horses of the
Polish army (ES). Some women were offered to take the train in
case they were tired, but these trains were taken directly to the gas
chambers (ES). The conditions at Birkenau are generally well-re-
membered after forty years, and each woman recounts the kinds
of details that caused some women—as all recalled—to commit
suicide by throwing themselves into the electric fence surrounding
the camp. There were constant roll calls during which the women
stood in rows of five. This is one of the few unanimously attested
details. These roll calls allowed the guards to keep count of the
prisoners and to ensure that none had escaped. JB says roll call was
from 3.30 am to 10 am, while another mentions it was at 5 am and
another that it was all day on Sunday (RF). RF also recalls that
they were naked during roll calls, at which time Mengele would
perform selections for the "hospital" (i.e., for experiments) or for
the crematorium. JB remembers that selections were performed
individually after roll call. Almost every woman mentions Mengele performing all selections, although they also hint that there
were, in fact, a dozen to two-dozen other doctors who performed
these. The women were given some coffee (JB), dark water (RG),
or so-called coffee but just brown liquid (LJ) after roll call. They
describe sleeping in beds of three stacks with six (JB), ten (BE),
or twelve (LJ, RG) to a bed. Although JB recounts the competi-
tion for survival and the fighting over resources, LJ reflects on the
self-sacrifice and the deep, even vital, solidarity of the women.[129]

LJ recounts that Anne developed scabies (a skin infection
caused by a burrowing mite) and was taken to the Krätzeblock
(the scabies barracks), yet RG remembers both Anne and Margot being sick and developing scabies (LJ later seems uncertain

about whether both were sick or just Anne). LJ recalls Margot volunteering to join Anne in the Krätzeblock; she also recalls Mrs. Frank's despair, and that Mrs. Frank dug a hole under the wall to feed her children bread. This conflicts slightly with RG's account, who says Frieda Brommet fed them bread which both her and Mrs. Frank stole for this purpose. Eventually, Anne and Margot were taken to Bergen-Belsen, while Mrs. Frank, too weak to travel, stayed behind to perish in Birkenau.

Overview

From these testimonies, we can draw together a consistent picture of this brief snapshot of Anne Frank's life from the time she left Westerbork throughout her stay in Birkenau. Her family left in a cattle car filled with people in terrible conditions on a trip to Auschwitz which lasted several days; upon arrival, there were spotlights, other prisoners in striped suits, and the first of many selections for the crematorium; Anne, like all other women and older girls, was stripped naked, tattooed, and began the regimented concentration camp existence of roll calls, selections, despair, and disease which led many women to commit suicide by throwing themselves against the electric fence surrounding the camp. Eventually, Anne contracted scabies and was tended to through her mother's means; when Anne and Margot were taken to Bergen-Belsen, they left their mother behind, who perished alone in Birkenau.

Aside from this general outline, there are many minor variations. Was the train ride one day, two days, or four days? How many people were in the cattle car? What color were the lights at Auschwitz? What time were the roll calls? How many women slept in a single bed? Did the women cooperate or compete for survival? Did Anne's mom give her bread in the Krätzeblock at Auschwitz, or was it Frieda Brommet, or both?

These differences do not take away from the overall picture but enhance its authenticity. Variations also tend to cluster around certain types of details, especially numbers of items, spans of time, colors, and which specific individuals were involved in certain actions.

EIGHT

Convergence

In the following four accounts, we see that Luke offers a slightly different perspective from Mark along the same lines as the differences found in the Anne Frank narratives. These variations occur in the same accounts that Luke scripturalizes, as discussed and surveyed in Chapter 6.

First, however, we must set our analysis more precisely against Luke's general treatment of Mark, which is very conservative. To press the point and to illustrate what I mean, Luke treats Mark with more reverence—i.e., he is less likely to alter, improve, or embellish Mark—than Josephus treats the Hebrew Bible.[130] Further, as Luke Timothy Johnson notes, although Luke takes over less of Mark's material than Matthew does, he is more conservative when it comes to changing Mark's accounts than Matthew is.[131] Second, our pattern must be appreciated against Luke's general editorial tendencies. Joseph Fitzmeyer highlights six editorial tendencies: first, Luke frequently improves Mark's Greek; second, Luke generally abbreviates Mark's stories by *eliminating* circumstantial or anecdotal details; third, Luke economizes his text by removing perceived duplicates; fourth, Luke deliberately omits source-material that does not move the reader toward Jerusalem as the story's climax; fifth, Luke transposes Mark's material for literary effect; sixth, Luke eliminates "the violent, the passionate, or the emotional."[132] Given Luke's conservative treatment of Mark in general and the nature of his editorial tendencies, we are going to see that in the accounts that Luke scripturalizes, he also does the *opposite* of what he typically does with Mark's text: he adds details, lengthens Mark's accounts, and adds emotional content, especially from the perspective of a named character.

The Calling of the First Disciples

Mark 1.16–18 and Luke 5.1–11 provide remarkably different perspectives on the calling of the first disciples. Mark simply recounts: "As Jesus walked beside the Sea of Galilee, he saw Simon and his brother Andrew casting a net into the lake, for they were fishermen. 'Come, follow me,' Jesus said, 'and I will send you out to fish for people.' At once they left their nets and followed him."

Luke adds a fresh block of material to Mark's text including: 1) Jesus teaching to a large crowd; 2) insights into Simon's business partnership with the sons of Zebedee; 3) specific details around Jesus' calling of these first disciples; 4) focused and vivid details around Peter's experience of a miraculous catch of fish: what he saw (v. 8), said (v. 3–5), felt (v. 9), and his realization of the lordship of Jesus (v. 8). These details then provide the explanation for Mark's comment that "at once they left their nets and followed him" (v. 18). Not only is the vivid "autopsy" (seeing for oneself) perspective present—which ancient historiographers aimed to glean from eyewitnesses—but the account provides the answer to the critical historical question: why would anyone suddenly leave everything to follow a stranger? Luke's scenario of a wildly charismatic teacher performing a personal, radical miracle before Simon and his companions provides such an answer.

Unlike Mark, Luke calls the Sea of Galilee "The Lake Gennesaret" in this text. As various scholars note, locals from the region of Galilee, according to Josephus, refer to the body of water as "The Lake Gennesar" (*J. W.* 3.463; cf. 2.573; 3.506; *Ant.* 18.28, 36),[133] the very toponym reflected in the NT only in Luke, who provides a Hebraic form of the name.[134] But Luke's use of "The Lake Gennesaret" is in this case not merely a passive reception on his part; he never deviates from using it to consistently replace Mark's "Sea of Galilee" throughout his Gospel. It appears that he has a reason for preferring the toponym, which could be explained by Josephus' comment that it reflects the local usage.

Luke includes several of the key Hebraic discourse markers in this text. ἐγένετο δὲ, as already noted, translates the Hebrew וַיְהִי (and it happened/came about), while ἐν τῷ τὸν ὄχλον ἐπικεῖσθαι (to be pressed by the crowd) is typical of the many Lukan uses of ἐν τῷ + infinitive in these Lukan additions, mirroring the בְּ plus the infinitive construct of the Hebrew Bible. That Simon "answered and said" (ἀποκριθεὶς ... εἶπεν) is also a well-known Semitic construction.[135]

The Transfiguration

Mark 9.2–13 and Luke 9.28–36 both relay Jesus' transfiguration. Immediately Luke alters Mark's text in terms of the timeline. While Mark indicates a six-day removal from the prior event (9.2), Luke remarks that it was "some eight days later" (9.28). Luke's account also contains many additional comments about Peter and is told from Peter's perspective, including supplemental insights highlighting Peter's emotions and reactions (what he saw, 9.32, 34; what he felt, 9.34). Luke adds details omitted by Mark: the transformation of Jesus' face; a different description of Jesus' clothing; the substance of Jesus' conversation with Moses and Elijah, etc. Rather than inserting a fresh block of material, as in 5.1–11, Luke weaves several new details into Mark's transfiguration narrative. The insertions contain the same Semitisms highlighted above but also Semitic variants of words (Ἰερουσαλήμ for Jerusalem) and the expression also very typical of Luke's discourse markers: καὶ ἰδού (and behold).

Luke likely supplemented Mark's text with extra material he received from an informant here, adorning it with a biblical narrative style that added weight and authenticity to this setting. Further, it would be difficult to explain why Luke is willing to vary from Mark on a detail such as how many days had passed (Mark 9.2; cf. Luke 9.28) or what was said (Mark 9.4; cf. Luke 9.30–33) unless he felt he had good grounds for improving the initial account, especially since this contradicts his typical editorial tendency with Mark. Such variations, however, are found in both ancient and modern accounts of independent eyewitnesses (more on this below).

The account is further pervaded by details that might interest an inquirer. One could readily imagine such an inquiry: "Are you sure about how much time had passed? Why did you go up the mountain in the first place? What did the two men talk about? Are you sure you were fully awake when you witnessed these things?"[136] The strength lies in the convergence of these variables—the Semitisms, the features of personal event memories, the Petrine perspective, and the historically interesting variations—to betray Luke's Thucydidean hand.[137]

The Blind Man in Jericho

Mark 10.46–52 and Luke 18.35–43 provide separate accounts of the healing of Bartimaeus. Mark's perspective focuses on Bartimaeus, while Luke's perspective focuses on the crowd.[138] Unlike

Mark, Luke mentions the *crowd* in v. 36 telling Bartimaeus that Jesus is passing by. Luke no longer finds the name "Bartimaeus" significant and drops it but adds that the crowd glorified and praised God in response to his healing (v. 43). Luke modifies Mark on the timing of the event, placing it during Jesus' arrival in Jericho (v. 35) rather than Jesus' *departure*, as in Mark 10.46.

Of interest is Luke's subsequent focus on Zacchaeus, someone Richard Bauckham suggests as a source behind Luke 19.1–10. Although Bauckham notes the vividness of the Zacchaeus narrative, he fails to connect it to the preceding and following scenes of which Zacchaeus could have naturally been a source as well.[139] This would explain the perspective of the crowd in Luke 18.35–43; if we take Zacchaeus' account at face value, it seems reasonable that Zacchaeus would recall the experience that first piqued his interest in Jesus. Jesus' entry into the city, accompanied by a public healing, could have prompted Zacchaeus' attempt to get a closer look from his sycamore tree—a curious detail, since these did not grow in the Northern Mediterranean at the time but were, according to the second-century rabbi Abba Shaul, very common to Jericho.[140]

Women at the Tomb

Luke's account of the empty tomb in 24.1–12 (L) varies in points not only with Mark 16.1–8 (M) but also Matthew 28.1–10 (Ma) and John 20.1–18 (J). Luke introduces this passage with his typical Semitic discourse markers (καὶ ἐγένετο; ἐν τῷ + infinitive). As noted in our fourth chapter, the various accounts show signs of independence. They concur that the women journeyed to the tomb on the first day of the week (J, L) after the Sabbath (Ma) very early (L) at dawn (Ma). J and M differ, however, as to whether it was just after sunrise (M) or while it was still dark (J).

All accounts name Mary Magdalene as one of the women while indicating the presence of other women (J mentions only Mary but implies others—John 20.2, οἴδαμὲν ποῦ ἔθηκαν αὐτόν, "*we* do not know where they have placed him"); Ma, L, and M also mention the presence of Mary the mother of James, while only M mentions Salome, and L adds Joanna "and others" while removing Salome. M mentions the women bringing spices to anoint the body, while L simply notes them bringing spices they had prepared; M, L, and J all mention that the women find the stone rolled away as they approach.

M recounts they then find a young man dressed in white, sitting on the right side in the empty tomb; this man gives them the message that Jesus has risen and has gone ahead into Galilee, where they should immediately follow. L recounts not one (as in M) but two men with bright clothes who say that Jesus has risen but mention nothing of a future appearance in Galilee; further, L does not indicate that the angels are sitting, although ἐπέστησαν in Luke 24.4 (from ἐφίστημι) does not necessarily indicate a standing posture and could refer to the angels' mere presence.[141] As in the accounts of Anne Frank after the *achterhuis*, these accounts portray a single picture with a divergent set of details.

All this is important because it is commonly believed by prosecutors, judges, and police officers that inconsistency between eyewitness testimony—whether by apparent contradiction, omission of detail, or commission of detail (adding details when questioned later)—is a sign of deception. The opposite is true. As a detailed, controlled study conducted by several Swedish researchers concluded: "In sharp contrast to this belief... statements produced by liars in collusion are more consistent than are statements produced by truth tellers who have experienced an event together."[142] In other words, minor variations and additional points of detail are the hallmark of testimonies that spring from different eyewitnesses.

Among historians there was also a tendency to differ over incidental details due to memory failings or to variant recollections from sources (cf. Suetonius, *Galba* 20.1; Tacitus, *Hist.* 1.43; Plutarch, *Galba* 26.5); sometimes ancient historians recount the more reliable version of an incident although this version works against their rhetorical aims (cf. Suetonius, *Otho* 9.1–2; Tacitus, *Hist.* 2.11–33).[143] The value of considering these modern and historiographical parallels is not to suggest that our analogy with the Anne Frank narratives can or must explain every feature of Luke's text that we have discussed. It does, however, weigh in favor of the probability that Luke did use eyewitnesses as sources, not only in the accounts surveyed but also more generally. This is supported by further incidental features of Luke's text. Luke goes out of his way, for example, to mention that the women were witnesses to Jesus' crucifixion and that they had followed Jesus from Galilee (Luke 23.49), just as he takes pains to name them in the beginning of Jesus' ministry (Luke 8.3) and toward the end of his Gospel (24.10). These women had been with Jesus *the whole time*, according to Luke, which is the very criterion he highlights for what it takes to be an authoritative witness to the gospel message (Acts 1.21–22).

None of what we have discussed excludes the possibility of literary creativity in the Gospels—in fact, it is Luke's literary creativity of scripturalizing these passages that tips his hand. These parallels merely set our thesis in the context of common and repeated experience, both ancient and modern.[144] One might suspect, for example, that written dependence—in our case, the dependence of Luke upon Mark and other possible literary sources—excludes the legitimacy of positing additional oral sources for the author. But even a brief look at historical practice would put this concern to rest. From all of Plutarch's works there is only one scenario wherein he may have relied on only a single source (the biography of Coriolanus), yet even when he used only one written source as his template, it was his general practice to supplement it extensively with other written and oral sources and to sift these critically.[145]

Explaining the Fractal Tell

This exercise has captured a fourth historical tell which I have labeled as a "fractal tell"; it draws everything we have discussed thus far together and involves the clustering of the following features in certain portions of Luke's text: names (see Chapters 2–4), vividness (see Chapter 5), Semitisms (see Chapter 6), but also signs of inquiry and features also found in the recollections from Holocaust survivors after a forty-year timespan (see Chapters 7–8). Are Luke's variations surveyed above *best* explained as features of eyewitness testimony? Several reasons suggest that they are, and at this point we revisit our comparison to the Anne Frank narratives.

First, the differences created by Luke's alterations occur around types of details that also vary in the Anne Frank narratives: issues of timing, numbers of items, personal perspectives, and minor details. Mark 9.2–13 and Luke 9.28–36, as noted, both relay Jesus' transfiguration, but while Mark indicates a six-day removal from the prior event (9.2), Luke remarks that it was "some eight days later" (9.28). Similarly, none of the witnesses to Anne Frank agree on the length of the journey from Westerbork to Auschwitz on September 3, 1944.

Second, the differences between the Anne Frank narratives, like the variations between Luke and Mark, occur especially in latent, vividly described situations wherein additional emotional and sensory details are added. On their arrival at Auschwitz, for example, only JB recalls the gate and the sign ARBEIT MACHT FREI ("work sets you free"). JB and LJ recall the loudspeaker, while most women comment on seeing prisoners in striped outfits (BE, LJ, RG) and oppressive lights which are described by different colors. Some cannot remember if it was morning or evening, while others recall that it was night. Likewise, Luke 9.28–36 contains many Petrine additions: the transformation of Jesus' face, for example, and a different description of Jesus' clothing. The accounts of the empty tomb, likewise, contain variations on the time of the morning and the number of angels described.

Third, Luke's variations from the Gospel of Mark lack correspondence to theological themes or expectations in Luke's Gospel, differing from Mark in theologically uninteresting ways. For example, it hardly matters whether Bartimaeus was healed while Jesus was entering or leaving Jericho or whether the transfiguration occurred six days or some eight days after the previously described event. This last change is particularly significant because in doing so, Luke *removes* a potential Mark/Matthew allusion to the six-day wait for Yahweh by Moses on Mt. Sinai (Ex. 24.16).

Fourth, Luke seems to lack sufficient reason not to harmonize with Mark in these accounts if not for the fact that he believed he had more immediate sources available in such cases. This is supported by Luke's exchange of "The Sea of Galilee" from Mark's text with "The Lake Gennesaret." The former appears to be a theologically motivated title used by the other Evangelists; the latter reflects the local usage.[146]

Fifth, the accounts consistently recall either first-person perspectives (esp. from Peter) or the names of minor participants in Luke's narrative (as in the accounts of the women and Zacchaeus). Variability in the recollection of names, as in the empty tomb narratives, is likewise a feature of the Anne Frank narratives. During the end of their stay in Birkenau, for example, LJ recalls Margot volunteering to join Anne in the Krätzeblock; she also recalls Mrs. Frank's despair, and that *Mrs. Frank* dug a hole under the wall to feed her children bread. This conflicts slightly with RG's account, however, who says *Frieda Brommet* fed them bread which both her and Mrs. Frank stole for this purpose.

Lastly, several points of interconnectedness like those between Luke and Matthew's Gospels (e.g., how Joanna's marriage to Chuza, called Herod's *steward* in Luke 8.3, explains Matthew's insight about Herod's servants in Matt. 14.2) can also be found in the Anne Frank narratives. Here I detail only two:

- During roll calls, Janny Brandes-Brilleslijper recalls having to stretch out her arms, without explanation, while Lenie de John-van Naarden incidentally mentions the reason: so that the SS could walk easily between rows.
- Hannah Elisabeth Pick-Goslar recounts speaking to Anne in Bergen-Belsen and occasionally throwing red cross packages to her; this explains why Rachel van Amerongen-Frankfoorder recalls Anne and Margot going to the fence line regularly, being sure that Anne knew someone on the other side (in what was called the "free" camp, where Hannah Elisabeth Pick-Goslar stayed).

These undesigned coincidences, as McGrew calls them (following James Blunt), are also created by ancient historians relying, as Luke does, on both written and oral eyewitness sources.[147] We will discuss several of these historical "coincidences" between Luke and John's Gospels in Chapters 10–11. Difficult to create in a work of fiction and difficult to hide in a historical work, Luke unintentionally proves the driving motivator of his writing—he cannot hide his hand. That Luke—*as a definitive pattern*—prefers information from eyewitness testimony is corroborated by the relationship between the Gospel of Luke and the "Beloved Disciple," and this segues into our last historical tell. It focuses on patterns between Luke and John yet also serves to illustrate how Luke's creativity as an author is not at odds with his respect for eyewitness testimony.

NINE

The Beloved Eyewitness [148]

The Gospel of John was once neglected as a historical source by New Testament scholars because it was so different from the Synoptics. John records three Passovers during Jesus' ministry verses only one. John, unlike the Synoptics, places the temple cleansing at the beginning of Jesus' ministry rather than at the end. John is also different in his emphasis on spiritual matters: in John's Gospel, Jesus makes more overt claims to be, for example, the embodiment of the temple, or even to be the "I am" (God's personal name, Yahweh) who revealed himself to Moses; beyond this, Jesus' message in John is more overtly evangelistic than in the Synoptics, and this message is communicated more simply and elegantly. [149]

A growing number of scholars, however, have begun to realize that John's Gospel is of considerable historical value. John provides his own version of events, to be sure, but these should not be discounted simply because they differ from the other Gospels. [150] It just means that the relationship between the Synoptics and John's Gospel is less like a rehearsed story; instead, John provides what is a bit more like an independent corroboration. The different portraits of Jesus presented by Luke and John are much like the famous "ambiguous images" of modern psychology. A prime example (see below) is William Ely Hill's 1915 illustration titled

"My Wife and My Mother-in-Law," with the caption: "They are both in this picture—find them."[151]

Most visualizers will first see a young woman in this illustration; she has her head tilted toward her right and away from the viewer. The interpretation of the image, however, is impacted by the background information of the observer. Older individuals are more likely to see the second possible image—the face of an older woman with a big nose looking straight ahead.[152] Once the viewer experiences the paradigm shift and sees both images, the brain can transfer between both interpretations. This process is also impacted by background considerations. Bilingual children, for example, are consistently more adept at making the dual identification and transfer, this again impacted by the ability of the brain to transfer from one paradigm to another.[153]

John's Gospel, likewise, may seem like a "paradigm shift" from the Synoptics. Yet, although Luke and John may create different perspectives, they still draw within the same lines. This discovery has tremendous value for appreciating the historical and spiritual connections between Luke and John. First, we will look at their *historical* connections; then in the following chapters we will examine some subtle similarities in their *theological* portraits of Jesus.

Historical Connections

Pierson Parker highlighted that the Gospels of Luke and John exclusively share many incidental features: a shared focus on several named persons (e.g., Mary and Martha of Bethany, Mary the mother of Jesus, etc.); a shared focus on Jerusalem, Samaria, the temple, the priesthood, and John the Baptist's ministry;[154] an allegedly shared historiographical interest, focusing on truth, testimony, and eyewitness criteria (c.f. Luke 1.2, Acts 1.21; John 15.27). Both Luke and John place Jesus' prediction of Peter's denial in the Upper Room as opposed to *en route* to the Mount of Olives, like the other Synoptics do. Matthew and Mark have Peter's second denial addressed to a servant girl, while Luke and John seem to agree together against this (Luke 22.60; John 18.25). Only the Gospels of Luke and John record that Peter cuts off a servant's *right* ear (Luke 22.50, John 18.10).

I give many more examples elsewhere.[155] The point is that these contribute to a larger pattern. According to Parker's analysis, John's Gospel sides with Matthew only twenty-six times, with Mark only nineteen times, and with Mark and Matthew together against the Gospel of Luke twenty-three times. *Yet Luke and John side together against Mark and Matthew 124 times.*[156] The areas of agreement occur almost entirely in the kerygmatic† portions of

---

† "Kerygmatic" refers to the earliest material proclaimed by the disciples of Jesus.

the traditions, the narratives concerning John the Baptist, Jesus' Passion (his final week), and his resurrection.

Another interesting feature—although unnoticed up to the present—is the link between accounts wherein Luke *prefers information* from John's Gospel and the places that *the Beloved Disciple* is said or implied to be an eyewitness in John's Gospel (1.35–40; 13.23–26; 19.25–27, 35; 20.2–10; 21.2, 7, 20–24). If we examine the nineteen sections, as noted by the biblical scholar Lamar Cribbs, in which Luke deliberately moves away from Matthew and Mark whenever John's Gospel provides an alternative reading, sixteen of these nineteen accounts occur in places that the Beloved Disciple is implied to be present in the Gospel of John.[157] This correspondence becomes more significant as we consider that the Beloved Disciple is only implied to be present in approximately thirty-two of the 879 verses in John's Gospel.[158]

What best explains this correspondence—specifically, what explains the fact that Luke seems to consistently agree with details from John's Gospel almost exclusively in the places wherein the Beloved Disciple is present?

Certainly, the best explanation is not that John used Luke's Gospel as a source. The Beloved Disciple is presented as a witness to key events in the Gospel of John (1.35–40; 13.23–26; 19.25–27, 35; 20.2–10; 21.2, 7, 20–24), and this presence corresponds to exactness of detail.[159] How strange it would be, in light of this, for the author of John's Gospel to rely on the Gospel of Luke almost entirely for the very events at which he places his key informant as eyewitness.

The best explanation also cannot be that Luke used John's Gospel as a source. In such a case, Luke chose to take over select portions about the Beloved Disciple while rejecting, without a trace, the Disciple's witness concerning the manner of Jesus' self-identity, his key theological imagery, the chronology of John's framework, large swaths of Jesus' discourses, and the general circumstances of even those accounts in which Luke and John share common features (Luke 9.10–20 vs. John 6.1–59; Luke 7.35–50 vs. John 12.1–11). It is possible that Luke had access to a primitive account of John's Gospel that only included those narrative portions in which the Beloved Disciple was present,[160] yet there are reasons to doubt this.[161] The internal evidence alone supports a more tangential relationship between Luke and John in which similar oral traditions were received and applied separately to various literary contexts.[162] Likewise, certain themes and focal points appear to have been jointly picked up, while others were left to develop independently, as we discuss in the following chapters.

Given that the strongest correspondences between the Gospels of Luke and John occur in just those portions focusing on eyewitness detail and within the earliest layers of the gospel proclamation (i.e., those portions that focus on the Baptist, the Passion, and Jesus' resurrection), it is conceivable that Luke acquired these at an early stage through a personal encounter with the Beloved Disciple. It is, of course, possible that this informant was not the Beloved Disciple himself but was a trusted companion who relayed the Disciple's testimony to Luke in person.

The suggestion that it was the Beloved Disciple himself, however, seems more plausible. The widespread preference in ancient history writing for living informants versus written accounts could explain why Luke consistently prefers John's versions of accounts to the Markan/Matthean counterparts. This also explains the correlation between these accounts and sections in the Fourth Gospel wherein the Beloved Disciple is present.[163] As time went on, both authors internalized and developed their shared narratives and, influenced by unique temperaments and experiences, drafted versions of their Gospels much closer to what we have today.

TEN

Acceptable

Given the conclusions of the last chapter, when could Luke and the Beloved Disciple have met? If Luke was a participant in the "we" sections of his Acts narrative (see Chapter 5), we must concede Luke's general familiarity with the very centers of ministry also attested to by the early church for the author of John's Gospel: Jerusalem (Clement of Alexandria, *Stromata* 6.5) and Ephesus (Irenaeus, *Haer.* 3.1.1, cf. *Hist. Eccl.* 5.8). The Church has long assumed that this author was John son of Zebedee, so it is interesting that this person is constantly named in Luke-Acts even when he plays no significant role (Luke 5.10, 9.54, 22.8; Acts 4.1–22, 8.14–15). In such cases Luke always couples Peter and John together, which is mirrored in the Fourth Gospel with Peter and the Beloved Disciple.[164]

Rainer Riesner, likewise, argues that John son of Zebedee was interviewed by Luke as one of the "eyewitnesses from the beginning" (Luke 1.2). Riesner observes:

> It seems remarkable that John begins to take the second place after Peter and before his brother James (Luke 8.51; 9.28; diff. Mark 5.37; 9.2; Luke 22.7) in the Gospel of Luke. This cannot solely be explained by John's later leading position next to Peter in the early Jerusalem community according to the Book of Acts (Acts 3.1–11; 4.1–22; 8.14; cf. Gal 2.9), because in some passages of his Gospel, Luke has preserved the traditional sequence (Luke

5.10; 6.14; 9.54). Astonishingly, John is always mentioned before James whenever we are given a description of those events where he could have served as a special witness.[165]

If Riesner is correct, John son of Zebedee could have played such a role for Luke's transfiguration narrative (Luke 9.28–36) alongside Peter (see Ch. 8). Just on the heels of this account is the deeply Semitic hinge of Luke's Gospel (9.51–56; see Figure 1), a text that divides Luke's narrative into two, which is also re-counted from the eyewitness perspective of the sons of Zebedee (Luke 9.54). This hinge introduces a lengthy section often called the "Lukan Travel Narrative" (Luke 9.51–19.44), or more precisely the "Great Interpolation" (Luke 9.51–18.15), because Luke adds this swath of text—which discusses Jesus' final trip to Jerusalem—*into* his template of Mark's Gospel wholesale. Luke's interplay between theological and historical concerns is acutely seen in this part of his Gospel. It also displays a particularly intriguing connection between Luke's and John's texts.

Luke's Travel Narrative is replete with apparent geographical problems. Most scholars no longer see it as a geographical endeavor by Luke.[166] David Gill in the 1970s, for example, makes the following comment: "In recent years scholars who have studied the problem have reached what may fairly be called a consensus that the Lukan Travel Narrative is primarily a theological-Christological rather than a geographical entity."[167]

This consensus has not diminished. Darrell Bock makes this remark thirty years later: "currently, the most popular view is that Luke arranged this section for theological purposes, so that a specific journey or set of journeys in some chronological sequence is not being presented."[168] The tenacity of this view is influenced by the difficulties involved in seeing a chronological, historical journey behind this account.[169]

In the early twentieth century, these problems played a central role in undermining the credibility of Luke's project. J. A. Robertson's statement reflects this position:

> There is no portion of the writings of Luke which presents a more forbidding obstacle to our acceptance of the claims of the evangelist to be an accurate and orderly historian than the section of the Third Gospel which is sometimes called "the Travel Narrative." It is the happy hunting ground of the detractors of the historian. And his defenders have sought to gloss over the difficulties that confront us here by suggesting that the "order" in which Luke declares he has arranged his material is logical rather than chronological.[170]

Luke begins Jesus' journey toward Jerusalem from Galilee in Luke 9.51, wherein Jesus steadfastly sets (ἐστήρισεν) his face toward the capital city. So far, so good. As Jesus travels, he enters Samaritan villages (9.52) while on the way to the home of Mary and Martha (10.38)—which John 11.2 identifies as Bethany, a small village to the southeast of Jerusalem. After this, Jesus travels through various unspecified places, villages, towns, and synagogues (11.1; 13.10, 22), and then he continues to "make his way toward Jerusalem" (13.22), perplexingly, to end up in Luke 17.11, "still on his way to Jerusalem," but back on the *northern border* of Samaria and Galilee, only to end up later in Jericho (19.11, where Luke geographically reconnects to his Markan template—see Figure 2 below).

The verb in Luke 9.51, στηρίζω, is otherwise translated in this context as Jesus "was determined [to go to Jerusalem]" (NASB), "resolutely set out" (NIV), "steadfastly set his face" (ASV). It communicates fixed resolve and determination of purpose. Luke's narrative reinforces this singular urgency on the part of Jesus by a repetition of peppered comments from the author that Jesus continues to be "on his way to Jerusalem" (9.53, πορευόμενον εἰς Ἰερουσαλήμ; 13.22, ποιούμενος εἰς Ἰεροσόλυμα; 17.11, πορεύεσθαι εἰς Ἰερουσαλήμ; 18.31, ἀναβαίνομεν εἰς Ἰερουσαλήμ; 19.28, ἀναβαίνων εἰς Ἰεροσόλυμα). Although this section is geographically and chronologically nebulous compared to the later travel narratives of Acts (cf., the "we" passages discussed in Chapter 5) this hardly avoids the impression that the author, who writes "with order and care" (Luke 1.3), wants us to believe that Jesus is on a real journey with his face toward Jerusalem.

Approaching the Travel Narrative from a historical as well as a theological perspective, we immediately see that a connection with the Gospel of John appears in Luke 10.38–42, where Jesus is said to visit the house of Martha and her sister Mary. John's rendition of Jesus' travels to Mary and Martha's house in the weeks preceding his death are as follows: Jesus travels from the Feast of Dedication in Jerusalem (John 10.22), to the East of the Jordan river (10.40), and then back to Bethany near Jerusalem (11.17–18), raising Lazarus and then retreating north to Ephraim (11.54).

Clearly, both Luke and John view these itineraries as final, fatal, and intentional on the part of Jesus.[171] For example, although both Evangelists envision these events as taking place sometime before Jesus' triumphal entry into Jerusalem (which ushers in the final days leading to Jesus' crucifixion), both Luke's Travel Narrative and John's Bethany Narrative directly precede Jesus' triumphal entry in each Gospel. If we place the journeys of Luke's Travel Narrative and John's Bethany Narrative on top of one another, we come up with a simple map (see Figure 2 below).

This map appears inconsequential on the surface. There is nothing indicating that Jesus took this trip because he "steadfastly set his face toward Jerusalem."

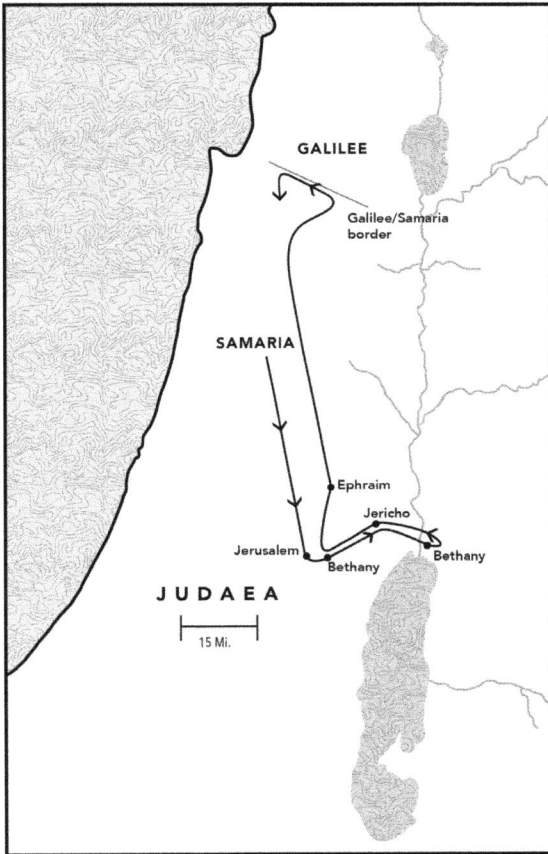

FIGURE 2

We do learn from Luke's Gospel, however, that Jesus views his "going up" to Jerusalem (Luke 9.51) in line with the prophetic tradition. This is especially emphasized in Luke's Gospel as being in the tradition of the Elijah/Elisha narrative as recorded in the Septuagint.[172] Thomas Brodie highlights the literary connection, for example, between the introduction to Elijah's ascension (2 Kgs 2.1) and the introduction to Luke's Travel Narrative: "what is essential is that, even though, within the Bible as a whole, there are indeed three other references to people being taken away (Enoch in Gen 5.24; and Elijah in 1 Macc 2.58 and Sir 48.9), there are no other biblical texts, apart from 2 Kgs 2.1 and Luke 9.51, which speak of the one who is soon to be assumed as journeying to the fated place."[173] The remark made by James and John son of Zebedee at the journey's beginning (Luke 9.51–56, esp. 9.54, "Lord, do you want us to call down fire from heaven and destroy them?") finds a direct parallel in the Elijah account (2 Kgs 1.10, 12, 14).

Just following these verses, another allusion to the Elisha/ Elijah story occurs in Luke 9.57–62. In 1 Kgs 19.19–21, Elijah finds Elisha plowing his field. Elijah asks Elisha to become his disciple, but Elisha requests that he first be allowed to kiss his father and mother goodbye, which Elijah permits (1 Kgs 19.20). Again, in Luke's account there is a man who wants to become a disciple of Jesus (Luke 9.61) but who first wants to say goodbye to his family. In this case, Jesus *does not* permit him but instead says, "No one who puts a hand to the plow and looks back is fit for service in the kingdom of God." These three points illustrate how Luke's travel narrative from its inception ties into the Elijah/Elisha narrative, showing its resemblance to it but also the superior nature of Jesus' final ministry compared to that of Elijah/Elisha.[174]

Let us consider very briefly the travels of Elijah and Elisha from the Hebrew Bible. The Elijah ascension story is found in 2 Kgs 2 but is bound up thematically and linguistically with the encounter between Elijah and Ahaziah just preceding it in 2 Kgs 1; it is possible, as Brodie argues, that Luke had both accounts from the Septuagint in mind when he crafted Luke 9.51–56.[175] The itinerary of the Elijah/Elisha journey is as follows: 1 Kgs 1 takes place entirely in Samaria with Elijah (1 Kgs 1.2; although Elisha's presence may be assumed, cf. 2 Kgs 2.25), after which Elisha journeys with him from Gilgal (2.1), down to Bethel (2.2), to Jericho (2.4), and across the Jordan (2.7). After Elijah's ascension to heaven, Elisha proceeds alone, crossing the Jordan (2.14), to Jericho (2.18), back through Bethel (2.23), up to Mt. Carmel (2.25), and returning to Samaria (2.25). If we place the route of the Elijah ascension account on a map, it appears, like Jesus' travel itinerary, inconsequential, aside from one remarkable feature: the two journeys are very similar indeed (see Figure 3 below; cf. Figure 2).

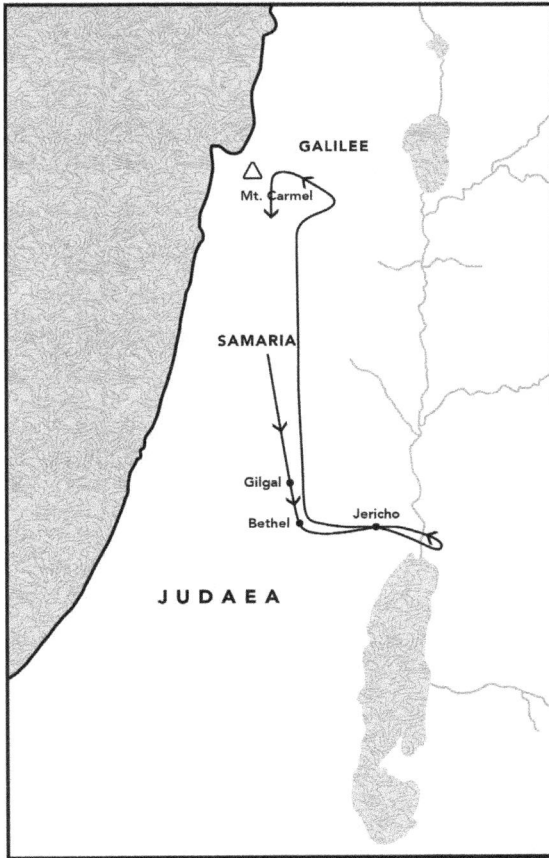

FIGURE 3

I have connected the locations in this figure, as in those of Figure 2, with direct lines indicating directionality but without reference to possible travel routes. This minimizes conjecture.[176] Looking at Figure 3, we can see that the differences in the journeys amount to two small points. First, some changes in townships/city locales emerge due to economic and cultural developments taking place between the second Iron Age and the Early Roman period in Palestine.[177] Second, Elisha specifically goes up to Mt. Carmel (1 Kgs 2.25), while Luke only says that Jesus travels along the border of Samaria and Galilee (Luke 17.11).

Luke's allusions to Elijah/Elisha traditions elsewhere in his Gospel become relevant at this point. The most important occurs in the account that we referenced in Chapter 1 (Luke 4.14–28), wherein Luke accurately describes the topography of Nazareth as a town built on a hill with a steep precipice. In this account, Jesus sums up his own ministry as follows, reading from Isaiah 61.1–2, the passage which introduces his activity throughout the Galilean ministry (4.31–9.50):

πνεῦμα κυρίου ἐπ᾽ ἐμέ, οὗ εἵνεκεν ἔχρισέν με εὐαγγελίσασθαι πτωχοῖς, ἀπέσταλκέν με κηρύξαι αἰχμαλώτοις ἄφεσιν καὶ τυφλοῖς ἀνάβλεψιν, ἀποστεῖλαι τεθραυσμένους ἐν ἀφέσει, κηρύξαι ἐνιαυτὸν κυρίου δεκτόν.[178]

The Spirit of the Lord is on me, because he has anointed me to preach good news to the poor, to preach release to the captives, to give eyesight to the blind, to send the oppressed away in freedom, and to preach a year that is to the Lord acceptable.[179]

I have intentionally translated this text quite woodenly. This passage is important because what happens next only makes sense if we treat the text within its authentic historical setting, assuming Luke's historical care. The recipients of Jesus' message find it to be one of tremendous grace (Luke 4.22), and their proclamation, "isn't this Joseph's son?" (4.22), cannot reasonably be read as a rejection of Jesus' covert claims of divinity (cf. Mark 6.2, Matt. 13.54). We would be reading this into the text.

The comment, instead, reflects the community's desire to seize Jesus' messianic good news for their own advantage.[180] Jesus' response in Luke 4.23, "Surely you will quote this proverb to me: 'Physician, heal yourself!' And you will tell me, 'Do here in your hometown what we have heard that you did in Capernaum,'" makes sense only within this setting. Jesus' comment, οὐδεὶς προφήτης δεκτός ἐστιν ἐν τῇ πατρίδι αὐτοῦ ("no prophet is *acceptable* within his hometown," 4.24), which differs from Mark (6.4) and Matthew (13.57) by replacing the οὐκ...ἄτιμος (not...without honor) with δεκτός (acceptable), likewise is not in reference to Jesus' *rejection* at Nazareth. Jesus is clearly not rejected in Luke 4.22 but is instead enthusiastically accepted by the people. Jesus goes on to compare his ministry to that of Elijah and Elisha, but neither were *they* rejected by the Israelites when God sent them to minister in Sidon and Syria, respectively, as Jesus goes on to highlight (Luke 4.26, 27).

Jesus' use of δεκτός (acceptable) in Luke 4.24 ties back to the final word in Jesus' Nazareth sermon. By cutting off the quotation from Isaiah abruptly, Luke emphasizes the word δεκτός ("acceptable," see my literal translation above). Jesus is likely not saying then, according to Luke, that no prophet is acceptable to his *own people* in his hometown, but rather that no prophet is acceptable *to God* in his hometown. In other words, the nature of a God-pleasing prophetic ministry like that of Elijah and Elisha is outward focused because a prophet of God is not bound by the borders of his hometown, just as the grace of God's message (cf. Luke 4.22, ...τοῖς λόγοις τῆς **χάριτος**) is free to extend to the unexpected recipient. Jesus is not Nazareth's prophet, but God's![181]

Such a consistent reading is only possible if we take Luke's historical setting seriously. Luke's Gospel strongly reflects this outward focus of Jesus' ministry and contains several more allusions to Elisha and Elijah's ministries. In the healing of a widow's son in Nain, Luke has Jesus not only mirror Elijah's miracle (Luke 7.11–17; cf. 1 Kings 17.10–24), but he inserts a Septuagint phrase verbatim: καί ἔδωκεν αὐτὸν τῇ μητρὶ αὐτοῦ ("and he gave him to his mother," Luke 7.16; cf. 1 Kings 10.24). Luke again demonstrates local knowledge here in describing the widow leading the funeral procession—a practice only followed in Galilean villages, but not in Judea/Jerusalem.[182] Evidently, Luke repeatedly ties his Elijah/Elisha motif to authentic historical situations, and this brings us to Luke's connection with John's Gospel.

The fact that this Elijah/Elisha-like journey of Jesus can only be reproduced by combining Luke and John's accounts is part of that large web of interconnectivity that we began to explore in the last chapter. Another is that both Evangelists portray Jesus as an Elisha-like figure. Gerald Bostock has noted, for example, that seven of Jesus' miracles in John's Gospel closely reflect the miracles of Elisha. Bostock notes other connections between Jesus and Elisha as well—not merely relating to Jesus' actions but also to his character—which span across the Canonical Gospels but are especially expressed in John's Gospel.[183]

What is to be said of this connection between the two Evangelists in how they portray Jesus? The link between the Septuagint's Elijah/Elisha account and the Gospel of Luke (esp. 9.51–56), coupled with the apparently undesigned recreation of the Elijah ascension account by Luke 9.51–18.14 and John 10.38–11.54, functions as a prime example of the potential historical and theological interplay in the Gospel of Luke. Earlier traditions likely existed which painted Jesus as an Elijah/Elisha figure who followed in the footsteps of his predecessors. A similar situation is mirrored in Matthew (e.g., Jesus' flight to Egypt to avoid the slaughter of the innocents, Matt. 1.13–23) and the Gospels elsewhere (e.g., the forty-day wilderness testing, Matt. 4.1–11; Luke 4.1–13) as they report Jesus retracing the steps of Moses. Such prophetic actions correspond with those of Jesus' near-contemporary, Theudas, who around 45 CE took his followers to the Jordan river, allegedly to watch him part it as Joshua once did (*Ant.* 20.97–99). Such actions were typical of the "Sign Prophets" of 40 CE to 70 CE, who may have taken their cue from Jesus' ministry.[184]

Further in Luke's travel section, Jesus' determination to "go to Jerusalem" (i.e., to his "exodus," 9.31), corresponds with an increase in Jesus' concern for the marginalized (e.g., the Parable of the Good Samaritan, Luke 10.25–35; 13.10–13; 14.11; 18.14; healing of the ten lepers, 17.11–19, etc.), an increase in his tension with the insiders (cf. Luke 10.13–15; 11.42–54; 13.14–17), and, therefore, an increasing proximity to his impending death, for "surely no prophet can die outside Jerusalem!" (13.33). If we take Luke's prologue at face value, that Luke crafted an accurate rendering (Luke 1.1–4), then this fatal Elijah/Elisha journey is a window into the life of the historical Jesus. It is possible that these links between Luke, John, and Elisha/Elijah are merely incidental, but it is worth our historical imagination. It adds weight to the likelihood that Luke had access to early traditions of Jesus and conserved primitive features while at the same time "scripturalizing," so to speak, the accounts that he received (see Chapter 6).

ELEVEN

Majestic [185]

Up to this point, we have focused mostly on Luke's unintentional features. These include naming practices that correspond to the apex of historical biographies (see Chapters 2–4), under which it was the general custom to use eyewitness sources when available (see Chapter 1). Chapter 5 demonstrated that Luke would have had ample opportunity to use eyewitness informants in his research, and Chapter 6 highlighted how Luke organized his eyewitness material through biblical tags to underscore the severe sacredness by which he esteemed them. These sacred accounts are nevertheless bound up with various historical tells that reveal Luke's interest in carrying on primitive traditions, leading to pointers of eyewitness testimony tracing back to the women who accompanied Jesus to Jerusalem, as well as traditions connected to Peter and John (Chapters 7–9). These first nine chapters demonstrated that Luke's use of eyewitness testimony is consistent with his historical tells and that it often provides the best explanation for their presence.

Chapter 10 began a subtle shift in focus. We continued the theme of Luke's relationship to John's Gospel from Chapter 9 but also noticed how Luke's reliance on eyewitness testimony and his literary creativity could be seen as complementary rather than contradictory. We looked specifically at Luke's Travel Narrative and interpreted it through Luke's focus on Jesus' Elisha-like ministry.

This present chapter and the next continue this type of investigation. These two final chapters demonstrate briefly how Luke, under the influence of such traditions, intended to write more than a biography of Jesus. He also intended to write a biography about God. Continuing our discussion from Chapters 9–10, we focus especially on connections to themes in the Gospel of John.

As mentioned in Chapter 9, John's Gospel is more open about Jesus' divinity, about the significance of the cross, and about the way Jesus embodied God's temple.[186] Luke is influenced by these ideas but artfully develops them in his own way. Since Luke is interacting with various eyewitness traditions, his picture of Jesus is multifaceted. Sometimes Jesus is depicted as an Elisha-like prophet (see our last chapter), sometimes as a Davidic king, sometimes as a second Moses, and sometimes as the Suffering Servant from the book of Isaiah. This is what we would expect if Luke were relying on multiple sources. The Beloved Disciple, if he is a source for Luke's Gospel, would be but one among many. Eyewitnesses like Jesus' mother and Peter, as we have discussed, could have played an equally vital role. Our emphasis here is that Luke's image of Jesus in the final product of Luke's Gospel has much in common with that found in the Gospel of John, although Luke's portrait is clearly faithful to other perspectives as well. Our first example comes from a passage on the heels of Jesus' arrest:

So Pilate asked Jesus, "Are you the king of the Jews?"

"You have said so," Jesus replied.

Then Pilate announced to the chief priests and the crowd, "I find no basis for a charge against this man." (Luke 23.2–4)

Luke's brief account is shocking and appears to be at odds with Roman law, which treated sedition as a capital offense. Even if we read Jesus' response in 23.2 in accordance with the NIV translation, "You have said so," and allow for its ambiguity, it is breathtaking that Pilate does not interrogate Jesus further and that he, without any apparent hesitation, declares Jesus' innocence. In this case, John's account fills in Luke's lacuna:

> Pilate then went back inside the palace, summoned Jesus and asked him, "Are you the king of the Jews?"
>
> "Is that your own idea," Jesus asked, "or did others talk to you about me?"
>
> "Am I a Jew?" Pilate replied. "Your own people and chief priests handed you over to me. What is it you have done?"
>
> Jesus said, "*My kingdom is not of this world* [emphasis mine]. If it were, my servants would fight to prevent my arrest by the Jewish leaders. But now my kingdom is from another place." (John 18.33–36)

In this instance, John's account incidentally explains the description of Pilate's actions as recorded in Luke 23.4.[187] But do we see the image of Jesus being a king "from another world" anywhere else in the New Testament? Well, yes, we see it woven throughout the early chapters of Luke's Gospel.

This early portion of Luke's text reflects a focus on Jesus as the promised Messiah, which is otherwise in line with the comments from Africanus (b. 180 CE), as quoted by Eusebius (*Hist. Eccl.* 1.7.14), that Jesus' family members were intent on preserving Jesus' genealogy, likely to prove Jesus to be the regal Son of David.[188] The titles of Jesus in this section, as spoken by the angel to Mary (1.32, "Son of the Most High"; 1.35, "Holy One," and "Son of God") while bearing an apparent flavor of the divine, would likely have been understood in strictly earthly terms by Mary, since such language was often used in antiquity to describe kings and emperors (see Figure 4 below). As we noticed in our

Introduction, Mary's personal insights in this passage mark her as a likely eyewitness to this narrative (see Luke 2.19, 51).

Several recent studies argue that Luke composed his Infancy Narrative as a counter-alternative to the birth accounts of Caesar Augustus.[189] Figure 4 below showcases the most relevant parallels:

Figure 4: Jesus-Augustus Parallels		
Topic	*Traditions About Jesus in Luke*	*Augustus Parallels*
Prophecy/portents pre-figure birth	1:26–38	Suetonius, Aug. 94
Miraculous conception	1.34–35	Cassius Dio 45.1.2
Cultic context	1.8–11	Suetonius, Aug. 94
Declared ruler/king at birth	1.32–33; 2.10–11	Suetonius, Aug. 94
Shepherds herald birth	2.8–20	Virgil, Ecl. 1:6–8
Birth is good news	2.10	Priene Inscription
Proclaimed Savior	2.11	Ibid.
Called Lord	2.11	Ibid., Acts 25:26
Bringer of age of peace	2.14	Ovid, Fast. 2. 127–44
Son of God	1.35	Tacitus, Ann. 1.11–13
Qualities at age twelve	2.41–52	Suetonius, Aug. 8

Although these parallels complement Mary's early regal perspective, Luke also uses them to accentuate the "other-worldliness" of Jesus in subtle ways. Unlike the despots of the Roman empire, for example, Jesus is born to a poor virgin. While Zechariah (1.5–9), Elizabeth (1.5–7), even Joseph (1.27), are imbued with pedigrees and descriptors of honor and cultural esteem in Luke's account—e.g., their old age, their cultic associations, their links to the priesthood, their lineages from Aaron and David—Luke's main character in these chapters, Mary, brings nothing to convey an esteemed status to Luke's audience.[190] Nevertheless, she is the focal point in conversation (2.34), is given words of prophecy (2.35), is granted unique insight (2.19, 51), and we are led to believe that God's blessing upon her is a reflection of a systematic *divine* reversal (1.46–55). A new type of kingdom emerges—God's upside-down kingdom.

Likewise, the Roman roads which bore the propaganda of the Roman empire are now being subjugated by the herald of the coming of the LORD (3.4–6), and even the worldwide census of Caesar Augustus serves ultimately to bring God's true king to the town God had promised, to Bethlehem (cf. 2.1).[191] Even a small detail like Luke's use of the term "Augustus" in 2.1 is revealing.

This is a transliterated form of the Latin title used for the Roman emperors.[192] Luke knows that the meaning of this title (which Luke treats as a meaningless name here in 2.1) is σεβαστός, commonly translated as the "majestic one" or "worshipful one." Commentators have neglected to ask why Luke uses the transliterated form here, especially since he otherwise translates the word (cf. Acts 25.21, 25). Further, Luke generally removes Latinisms,[193] and no other Greek writer for several hundred years uses this transliterated form, Augustus (Αὐγοῦστος), that Luke uses.[194] The likely explanation is that Luke refuses to translate the word into Greek for his audience because he is trying to emphasize the worshipfulness and majesty of *someone* in this text—but it is not Augustus. It is, rather, a baby born in a manger (Luke 2.7).[195] This baby is by Simeon referred to as the ἀνατολὴ ἐξ ὕψους (Luke 1.78, lit. "the sunrise from on high"), which, as Simon Gathercole has observed, is a veiled reference to pre-existence.[196] Jesus' sonship, Luke hints, goes beyond the regal and appears to have familial implications for his relationship to God (e.g., Luke 2.49).[197] Again, the Baptist prepares the way for Jesus in the fulfillment of Isaiah 40.3–5 (cf. Luke 3.4–6) which speaks of a forerunner preparing the way for *Yahweh*.[198] Although Luke tells this narrative through the messianic expectations of Mary, we are left with a picture much like John's: that Jesus is not from this world.

This "other-worldliness" of Jesus accentuates the literary contrast that Luke makes: while Caesar Augustus was adopted to become the Son of God (i.e., the son of the dead deified Julius) through oppression and exploitation, Jesus became a son of man through his implicit adoption by Joseph (Luke 3.23) as an act of humility. Jesus is a lover of the outsider and the marginalized, as we also discussed in our last chapter. But this characteristic is not a concession of Jesus. It does not occur *despite* who he is. It is an *outworking* of his identity as it is established in Luke's narrative which is—at this point in Luke's account, however subtly—shared with the God of Israel.

TWELVE

Theography

Having focused on Mary's perspective in the last chapter, let us now consider a section in Luke's Gospel from Peter's perspective. This section (4.31–9.50) neatly fulfills the parameters of ministry laid out by Jesus in Luke 4.18/Isaiah 61.1–2, a text we discussed in Chapter 10: to proclaim good news to the poor, freedom for the oppressed, recovery of sight for the blind, etc. The messianic nature of these activities and their accomplishment by Jesus are echoed again in Luke 7.22, in which Jesus responds to a question from John the Baptist about whether Jesus is the Messiah. Jesus says, "Go back and report to John what you have seen and heard: the blind receive sight, the lame walk, those who have leprosy are cleansed, the deaf hear, the dead are raised, and the good news is proclaimed to the poor."

This section, which occurs in between Jesus' sermon in Nazareth and Luke's Travel Narrative, is bracketed by accounts focused on Peter: Peter's initial call (Luke 5.1–11) and then his experience of the transfiguration (9.28–50), sections which both contain features of eyewitness testimony, as discussed in Chapter 8. Two things are important to observe. First, the perspective in this section is quite different from that found in Luke 1–4. Jesus *overtly* takes on the prerogatives of Israel's God in almost *every feature* by which he defines his messianic prerogative, as outlined by Luke 4.18/7.22, whether through word or through deed. For example, Jesus commissions Peter in the same manner that Israel's God commissioned Isaiah (cf. Is 6.1–8).[199] He forgives sins as the LORD forgives sins (Luke 5.17–26, 7.44–50). He has authority over Sabbath regulations as established by Yahweh (Luke 6.1–11), and in a staccato-like fashion he demonstrates his authority over death, disease, nature, and evil within a span of four short accounts (8.22–56).

This sudden, sharp emphasis on Jesus' divine identity is only our first observation. The more exceptional feature is the general thrust of Luke's account here. Peter's experiences do not move the reader *from* seeing Jesus as a prophet *to* seeing Jesus on par with Yahweh. The audience is confronted with Jesus' divine association *at the instance* Peter is commissioned by his Lord (Luke 5.1–11). The experiences within the narrative build toward a climax in the revelation of Jesus' identity, which is seen in the transfiguration (9.28–36).[200] This account, as we have noted, is of supreme importance to Luke. Not only does he add significant details to Mark's account, but it marks the main transitionary event prior to Luke's narrative of Jesus' travel toward his death (9.51–19.44).

As others have noted, Luke removes any doubt that the transfiguration should be equated with a theophany (a vision of God) of greater significance than Moses' experience at the top of Mt. Sinai.[201] Luke adds these key components into his recollection: the sense of glory (9.31–33, esp. Jesus' glory, 9.32), the focus on Jesus' ascent (9.28), the descent of the cloud (9.34), the fear of the disciples (9.34), and the shining face of Jesus (9.29).[202] Luke also reverses the Greek text of Mark's ἀκούετε αὐτοῦ (Mark 9.7) into αὐτοῦ ἀκούετε (Luke 9.35) in the Father's command concerning Jesus: "This is my beloved son, *listen to him*." Luke's alteration of the Greek wording does not translate into English, but it causes the words to match the Septuagint reading of Moses' words from Deut. 18.15 more precisely: "The Lord your God will raise up for you a prophet like me from among you, from your fellow Israelites. You must *listen to him*." Luke emphasizes Jesus' identity as a prophet greater than Moses.[203]

All of this is, surprisingly, only the window dressing. Embedded within the Father's command to Jesus' disciples at this point is a subtle change of only a single word from Mark's text: my *beloved* son (ἀγαπητός, Mark 9.7) to my *chosen* son (ἐκλελεγμένος, Luke 9.35). This change is as artful as it is revealing, because it designates Jesus' messianic identity explicitly in terms of the Isaianic servant of Isaiah 42.1 (LXX, ὁ ἐκλεκτός μου).[204] To this alteration is added Luke's comment that the topic of discussion was Jesus' upcoming suffering and death, his exodus (ἔξοδος, 9.31), so that what is both echoed and anticipated by the command "listen to him!" is Jesus' increased identification of himself with a certain type of messianic identity: the Suffering Servant of Isaiah. What is important in all of this, again, is the movement of the text. More overtly than Luke 1.1–4.30 (which is focused around Mary and Jesus' familial roots), Luke 4.31–9.50 (which is focused around Peter and the early disciples) moves *from* divine identity *to* servant identity. The new, surprising twist in the story is not Jesus' divine connection. Jesus' divine lordship is not a development out from his messianic status. The type of messiah that Jesus is destined to be—a crucified, self-sacrificial one, whether regal or prophetic—is a development out from divine lordship.

This theme is developed most clearly throughout the next section, Luke 9.51–23.47, where Luke shows the strongest historical connections to John. It is well-demonstrated in the culminating verse by the centurion's comment at Jesus' death.[205] The centurion states: "Surely this man was righteous/innocent (δίκαιος, Luke

23.47)," an implicit reference to Is. 53.11.[206] But both Mark 15.37 and Matthew 27.54 record the centurion's comment as follows: "Surely this man was the Son of God!" The question we must ask is this: what did Jesus' death demonstrate? Was it that he was the Son of God (Mark 15.37, Matt. 27.54)? Or was it that he was the righteous/just servant (Luke 23.47)? All that we've discussed leads us to Luke's likely answer, which would have been "Yes" to both. On the one hand, Luke honors and emphasizes the perspective also found in Mark's Gospel, that Jesus' ministry—leading into his eventual death/resurrection—proves his divine status, that Jesus is more than human. Yet Luke also incorporates a nuance more accentuated in the Gospel of John, that Jesus' divine servanthood, which led to his death, reveals the true character of God.

God's gracious character, for example, is demonstrated by Luke as Jesus meets ten lepers while traveling toward his death in Jerusalem (Luke 17.11–19).[207] Nine are Israelites while one is a Samaritan. Like John's account of Jesus and the woman at the well in John 4.1–26, the Gerizim temple and the proper place of worship lie in the background of the context.[208] In Luke's account, Jesus heals the ten lepers and tells them to go and "show yourselves to the priests" (17.14). Only one leper, the Samaritan, returns, and when he does so he worships at Jesus' feet (17.15–16). Jesus then makes a stunning, albeit cryptic, remark. He says what appears to be an ill-mannered statement (17.18): "Has no one returned to give praise to God except this foreigner (ἀλλογενὴς)?" ἀλλογενὴς is a completely unique word in the New Testament and is a term exclusive to Jewish literature. It occurs prominently in one place within Jewish antiquity: upon the signs that separated the Court of the Gentiles in the Jerusalem temple from the sacred space reserved only for Jews. These were the inscriptions that forbade any "foreigner" from entering upon the pain of death.[209]

Jesus appears to consider this leper's encounter with *him* as a substitute for the temple, whether in Jerusalem or on Mt. Gerizim. But Jesus here, unlike the Jerusalem temple, receives the Samaritan's worship at his feet as an expression of the leper's healing/salvation (17.19). Is this so different from what the Gospel of John tells us? Consider John 2.19–21:

> Jesus answered them, "Destroy this temple, and I will raise it again in three days."
>
> They replied, "It has taken forty-six years to build this temple, and you are going to raise it in three days?" But the temple he had spoken of was his body.

This shared emphasis between John and Luke is highlighted again by the parables of Luke 15, each of which relates to the other and is designed to highlight the prodigal nature of God, who loves ἀσώτως (prodigally, i.e., with self-abandon, recklessly). Trevor Burke highlights this emphasis in opposition to the traditional focus on the prodigal nature of the son in Luke 15.11–31 (the traditional title being based on ζῶν ἀσώτως in 15.13).[210] Indeed, each parable has its focus—whether on the shepherd (15.3–7), the woman (15.8–10), or the father (15.11–31)—on the one who receives the glory and the benefit of retrieving their lost items.

Kenneth Bailey argues that the issue of atonement is presented in story form within these parables, esp. in Luke 15.11–31.[211] Given the context of the honor-shame culture of Jesus' environment, each act that the father does in approaching his lost son—for example, of running for him, which would involve hiking up his garment, 15.20 (a humiliating act); granting him his signet ring, 15.22; giving him the best robe (his own robe), 15.22; and giving a great banquet, 15.23—is merely another sacrifice of degradation and personal abandonment. As Bailey shows, these acts occur apart from his son's repentance and are, therefore, unconditionally given over.[212]

Maarten Menken makes another point. The verb describing the father's response to seeing his lost son, that he "felt compassion" (ἐσπλαγχνίσθη, Luke 15.21), occurs as the central verb in Luke 15. This verb, whenever it occurs in Luke's Gospel, occurs in the center—in the literal center—of a given account; in these accounts, compassion marks the epitome of Luke's depiction of Jesus.[213] Luke 15, according to Bailey, is in itself Jesus' invitation to his interlocuters to receive the grace of God.[214] In the setting of Luke's Gospel, however, it is not God's actions that are being questioned, but rather Jesus' actions of eating with and welcoming sinners and tax collectors (15.1–2). Jesus, nevertheless, answers an accusation against *himself* with a three-fold set of parables about what *God* is like. The thrust of the message is undoubtedly echoed in much of John's writings, as Bailey explicitly notes:

> Some of the same theological meaning here created by parable [of Luke 15.11–31] is affirmed in other NT writings using other language. In the parable the father as head of the house and the father at the edge of the village are one person. In John's gospel Jesus says, "The Father and I are one" (10.30). Also in the parable the father becomes a suffering servant in order to reconcile his son to himself. St. Paul writes, "God was in Christ reconciling the world unto himself" (2 Cor. 5.19 KJV). What is said conceptually in John and in 2 Corinthians appears metaphorically in Luke 15.[215]

Surely Luke tells the story of God's Messiah through eyewitness perspectives like those of Mary, Peter, and others, but it carries the same undertone as John's text. The "Word" of John's prologue is defined as the one-of-a-kind Son (1.17, 18) who "exegetes" the Father. The Word does not merely make God known (according to the common term, γνωρίζω), but the Word draws out the message of God (according to the rare term, ἐξηγέομαι). This term is unique to John's prologue, and its Lukan occurrences (Lk 24.25; Acts 10.8; 15.12, 14; 21.19) give the sense of "giving a complete account." God's story is told completely, according to both Luke and John, in the person of Jesus.

Ambiguous Images

As we have looked at Luke's fifth tell—at subtle patterns of similarity between Luke and John—we also pointed out how various eyewitnesses possibly shaped Luke's biography of Jesus. These chapters synthesized previous findings about Luke's connection to individuals like Mary and Peter. These influences likely shaped Luke's composition; yet Luke, using the categories of these traditional sources (i.e. categories such as Davidic messiah, Moses-like prophet, suffering servant, etc.), sketches a subtle image that can be visualized as—and that cumulates to become—a biographical depiction of Israel's God. Luke's Gospel, too, is like the "ambiguous images" of modern psychology in this way. First, Luke draws the contours of Jesus' identity through the traditions of eyewitnesses. Second, he increasingly and consistently infuses the narrative with additional pointers to highlight how the parameters of divinity, as they were defined by Jewish understandings/expectations, are filled out by Jesus in the experiences of these eyewitnesses. In other words, Luke paints not merely a picture of Jesus (cf. a young woman), but through his portrait of Jesus creates a robust impression of Yahweh (cf. the mother-in-law). Here we notice how a sensitivity to Luke's use of eyewitness materials enriches our understanding of what we might call his "theography" —that is, of a biography that presents a new, creative portrait of Yahweh as much as it does a historical, faithful portrait of Jesus.

Conclusion

On November 25, 1960, JFK Jr., "John John," was born to the victor of a tremendous presidential campaign.[216] On January 20, 1961, his father became the youngest US president in history, while John John became the youngest First Child in approximately eighty years. In 1880, Queen Victoria had gifted President Rutherford B. Hayes with a desk crafted from the salvaged oak timbers of an Arctic exploration vessel called the HMS Resolute. It is called the "Resolute Desk." On January 20, 1961, it became what John John called "my house." The panel on its underside became "my secret door."

In the fall of 1963, a former photojournalist took several iconic photographs of John John in the Oval Office. One captures the toddler under the desk as JFK meets with a group of stern-faced politicians. The scene is marvelous. There in the center of the picture is that most magnificent, luxurious desk. And there, on the side, are the most powerful of men. It is difficult to imagine the heights of power these men have acquired. They encircle JFK. They embody greatness. Yet in the eyes of the camera, they are quietly subverted. Behind them, as the photographer snaps his photo, is John John in *his house*; he plays under the desk of power, taking center stage. He undermines political greatness.

This brief book has captured how the Gospels and especially the writings of Luke crawled onto the stage of history in that small, intrusive way. Luke somehow achieved naming patterns as vast and sophisticated as the most historically oriented biographies of ancient Caesars, and yet Luke's Gospel—written about a homeless Palestinian preacher named Jesus—introduced the triumph of a subversive kingdom. Today, as others have quipped, we name our guard dogs Brutus, Caesar, and Rufus; we name our children Peter, Mary, and John. President Kennedy, too, called his son John John and not Nero.

The aim here has been to make a positive, corroborative evidence case based on some new lines of evidence. What weighs in favor of the likelihood that Luke told the truth? What weighs in favor of the claim that he contacted eyewitness sources to compose his Gospel? We have looked at several features that show his hand:

- The intricate naming patterns found in the Synoptic Gospels that are only found in ancient historical works relying on archival information,
- The vividness in the "we" sections of the book of Acts, concentrated around the author's personal experiences such as those of Acts 27,
- The correspondence of biblical tags in Luke's Greek with the presence of named individuals in his text,
- Fractals of features that support eyewitness testimony whenever Luke deviates from Mark's text in minor ways,
- Subtle points of connection between the Gospels of Luke and John.

These features come together to create a corroborative evidence case; not only are they independent strands within a rope, but the threads of one argument often simultaneously thicken one or several of the other strands. For example, Luke's tendency to prefer material from the Beloved Disciple to that of his written sources (Tell 5) corroborates the case that Luke does the same elsewhere when he deviates from Mark's text in terms of minor detail (Tell 4). Luke's tendency to add the names of John son of Zebedee and Simon Peter to accounts wherein he makes these changes strengthens the case that Luke's names often functioned as living footnotes (Tell 1). Tendencies to recall accounts differently, as discussed under Tell 4 and in our investigation of the Anne Frank narratives, not only corroborates the Gospels' uncanny ability to recall names accurately (Tell 1), but it also sheds light on the especially vivid recall of Luke's shipwreck (Tell 2). Not only does this account in Acts 27 place Luke in the presence of Paul, but it also demonstrates his commitment to accuracy as well as the likelihood that he already saw himself as a historian of the early Jesus movement.

These tells not only place Luke within the proximity of living sources, but they demonstrate his likely commitment to the historian's ideal of engaging, whenever possible, with living informants.

In the process of observing Luke's historical care, we noticed something more. Luke's image of Jesus is an ambiguous image. That is, if we look at Luke's Gospel through a historical lens, we see a conservative portrait of Jesus; yet, if we read it through the perspective and expectations of the Jewish Scriptures, we notice that this very portrait is haunted by another image—the image of God Himself. On one level, Luke's Gospel answers the question, "What is Jesus like?", with the following answer: "He is more than a human." But on another level, his Gospel answers the question, "What is Yahweh like?", with the answer, "Jesus."

At the time when Luke wrote his Gospel, the fastest growing religion throughout the Roman Empire was the worship of the Roman Emperors. They were called Savior and Lord, and they were celebrated for bringing their gospel.[217] These lords ruled by conquest and might. Luke's Gospel challenges this perspective with the message of Jesus. This Lord is a seeker. This Lord is a servant. This Lord confronts greater, shared enemies: our death, our disease, our sin, our alienation. Perhaps Luke's story of God tells us something about ourselves as well. Do we need another godlike king? One who slaughters enemies and crucifies dissenters? No. Instead, Luke would argue, we need a kinglike God. But not like a king who is distant. We need one who is prodigal—wasteful, lavish—in his grace. One who meets Samaritans and saves them, who turns fishermen into evangelists. One who places his Son in Mary's borrowed manger. One who tells his story through women and men like us. And beneath the intricate layers, the Semitisms, the rich historical details, and the memories of eyewitnesses winks the undeniable conclusion: Luke told this particular story because this story was true.

APPENDIX A

Personal Names in Comparable Sources

This appendix provides the technical foundation for the discussion in Chapter 2.[218] It includes an overview of the relevant reference works, of naming patterns in antiquity, and of the onomastic features of twenty-three extrabiblical texts. Statistics on the usage of personal names within a composition cannot be acquired through systematic computer analysis; rather, each name must be catalogued while combing through each work individually. Unintentional errors in counting can occur. Michael Strickland, for example, highlights Bauckham's error in ascribing the name "Eros" to four persons in the Gospels-Acts, although Bauckham here is clearly incorrect.[219] Such a blunder is, in my estimation, not a reflection of the scholarly care (or lack thereof) of Dr. Bauckham; rather, it reflects the tedious, challenging process previously described.

This project is further complicated by other considerations: do we include nicknames? Demes? Patronyms? In my case I have opted to include names that seemed standardized to the extent that they could stand alone.[220] Of course, this process involves some subjectivity. Nevertheless, I am confident that the broad patterns of data represented by my research will not be changed by minor variations in counting.[221]

Several reference works are indispensable for determining onomastic congruence. These lexical sources, like telephone books, include lists of ancient names but also lists of persons bearing each name, often with relevant biographical details. They are onomasticons in the former sense and prosopographies in the latter, but for our interests I simply refer to them as "prosopographies."[222] Five are referenced:

- The *Lexicon of Greek Personal Names* (LGPN), now published in five volumes, catalogues approximately 36,000 Greek names from 345,000 ancient persons along the northern Mediterranean.[223] A sixth volume to include Palestine is forthcoming. Published volumes can be searched digitally.
- The *Prosopographia Imperii Romani* (PIR) covers 15,000 elite persons living in the Roman Empire from 31 BCE to 305 CE.[224] It is digitized by the Berlin-Brandenburgische Akademie Der Wissenschaften.
- The *Digital Prosopography of the Roman Republic* (DPRR) catalogues 4800 elite members of the Roman Republic from 509 BCE to 31 BCE.[225] It is digitized by King's College, London.
- The *Trismegistos People* database can also be searched digitally; it contains 33,900 names of 368,000 ancient persons living in Egypt and is based on the *Prosopographia Ptolemaica* (ProsPtol).[226]
- The last prosopography is Ilan I, covering 2953 occurrences of 521 names and available only in printed copy.[227] I will narrow her list to an onomastic snapshot of Jesus' Palestinian environment (30 BCE–90 CE). This timeframe generally captures persons living circa 30 CE; life expectancy was in the mid-twenties in first century Galilee, but only fifty percent lived to the age of five; after this, attrition rates level, with only ten percent living beyond sixty.[228]

Naming Practices

Naming conventions among ancient women differed from those among men. During the Roman Republic, women were generally deprived of a personal name; in ancient Athens it was against etiquette to mention a woman's name in oratory, and she was typically referred to only in relationship to a named father, husband, etc.[229] All female Latin names in Ilan I are derived from male names, with the simple addition of a female suffix (a). To give a sense of the disproportionate attention given to male names, it is worth noting that among the 2826 named persons in Ilan I (both fictional and nonfictional), only 317 are women: i.e., 11.2%.[230] Such androcentrism is pervasive, and therefore the naming practices of males—and often, of elite males—provide the broadest data for statistical analysis, and our study interacts primarily with them only due to their statistical prominence in both the relevant narratives and prosopographies. Ancient Greek and Jewish males were typically given one name. This name was qualified most frequently by the patronym in the genitive case, where υἱός is sometimes supplied: Σώπατρος Πύρρου (Acts 20.4), Φείδωνος υἱὸς Στρεψιάδης (Aristoph. Nub. 1.134).[231] The primary name could also be qualified by deme (Ἀριστάρχου Μακεδόνος Θεσσαλονικέως, Acts 27.2), by nickname (Σίμωνος τοῦ λεπροῦ, Mark 14.3), or by other means.[232]

The Roman naming system among elite males is comparatively complex. They typically had three names: the tria nomina. The first, the praenomen, was a personal name bestowed at birth; during the Republic ninety-nine percent of males shared only seventeen praenomina.[233] Due to this shared commonality, praenomina were eclipsed in public usage by the second name: the nomen.[234] Since the nomen was the family or clan name, males were individuated by their praenomen within the household but publicly by their nomen. Greeks struggled to assimilate this practice, however, and might refer to a public individual by the prae-nomen (e.g., to T. Quinctius Flamininus as "Titus"); due to the limitations of the praenomen, the cognomen—a third name—emerged as a popular alternative to qualify the nomen.[235] Since the cognomen was another personal name but far more versatile and well-suited, the nomen and cognomen together become the most common occurrence of named persons, for example, in Tacitus. Praenomina were simply abbreviated or excluded in Roman literature; therefore, the cognomen and nomen are the most relevant for determining onomastic patterns.[236]

To demonstrate these naming practices, a brief list of famous Roman persons and their *tria nomina* are given below in Figure 5; names by which these persons are generally known are italicized.

Figure 5—Roman Names		
PRAENOMEN	NOMEN	COGNOMEN
M. (Marcus)	Tullius	*Cicero*
G. (Gaius)	Julius	*Caesar*
T. (Titus)	Flavius	*Vespasianus*
T. (Titus)	Flavius	*Domitianus*
M. (Marcus)	Junius	*Brutus*

Onomastic Congruence in Comparative Sources

Onomastic analysis of twenty-three extrabiblical compositions reveals that onomastic congruence is only found in certain biographies from the Early Empire.

Apocryphal Gospels

The apocryphal gospels are the least persuasive in terms of onomastic congruence. The Infancy Gospel of Thomas, as mentioned in Chapter 2, has eight names, with Thomas the Israelite (Θωμᾶς Ἰσραηλίτης) as the only qualified name; aside from this unnatural qualification, a Palestinian Jewish boy is named Ζήνων, a name quite common in Delos and Athens but unusual for a Palestinian Jewish child.[237] The Gospels of Peter, Mary, and the Infancy Gospel of James have no qualified names and average less than ten names per work.[238] The Gospel of Nicodemus is the most robust with forty-six names, nine of which are qualified; these belong to public figures contemporaneous to the author, however, or known from the NT. One notable exception occurs in the prologue, missing in some MSS: Joseph Caiaphas. This first name is accurate and found nowhere in the canonical literature. As noted in Chapter 2, other names are positively incongruous: six of twenty-two allegedly Jewish names are unattested in Ilan I (Σήμης, Δαθαης, Νεφθαλείμ, 1.1; Αντώνιος, Αστέριος, Αμνής, 2.4) as well as the names of the two thieves crucified beside Jesus (Δυσμᾶς and Γέστας, 9.5).[239]

Apocryphal Acts

The apocryphal Acts achieve more complex naming patterns, yet these too lack onomastic congruence.[240] Although several names are qualified, there is no relationship between commonality of names and the presence of qualifiers. To illustrate, Barsabas Justus of the Broad Feet, Urion the Cappadocian, and Festus the Galatian—"Caesar's chief men"—are qualified in the Acts of Paul (10.2); Βαρσαβᾶς, however, is a Jewish name unattested in Roman prosopography while Ωρίων and Φῆστος, allegedly Greek, are very rare in the LGPN I-V (twelve and four attestations respectively, with zero attestations in either Cappadocia or Galatia). Second, there is an unusually high percentage of rare Greek names; for example, the Acts of John has five unique Greek names—Κλέοβις, some MSS Κλέοβιος; Δρουσιανή; Ἀριστοβούλα; Τέρτυλλος; Φουρτουνάτος—out of a total of only sixteen Greek names. Lastly, the Acts of Peter (2.26–33) names Agrippa as prefect in Rome, while no urban prefect ever bore the name of the familiar Judean client king; this Agrippa allegedly has four concubines—Ἀγριππῖνα, Νικαρία (only attested as a Greek island), Εὐφημία, and Δορις—the latter three Greek names almost completely unattested.

Novels

Extant ancient romances, including Longus' *Daphnis and Chloe*, Chariton's *Callirrhoe*, Achilles Tatius' *Clitophon and Leucippe*, and Heliodorus of Emesa's *Aethiopica*, anticipate the modern historical novel. *Daphnis and Chloe* contains twenty-six names, none of which are qualified and many of which are rarely attested in the LGPN I–V;[241] further, none but two are attested in Lesbos, where the story takes place.[242] *Callirrhoe* has twenty-seven names. Six are qualified by deme, but there is no apparent relationship between the qualification of the name, its local setting, or its popularity; it appears to be a random feature of the text.[243] *Clitophon and Leucippe* contains twenty-nine names, seven of which (twenty-six percent) are extremely rare, and it introduces several Egyptian persons with names more prominent in the LGPN I–V than in ProsPtol.[244] This situation is worsened in *Aethiopica* where three of its twenty-one names are supposedly Egyptian (Ὀρουνδάτης, *Aeth.* 2.24; Μιτράνης, 2.24; Χαλάσιρις, 2.35) but are unattested in either ProsPtol or the LGPN I–V. Although historical novels can succeed in planting traces of verisimilitude, of "generic markers of factuality," they fail to achieve onomastic congruence. Onomastic congruence seems to be a disturbing "intensely (even boringly) realistic" feature of a text which makes it "difficult to sustain the classification [of fiction]."[245]

In *Cyropaedia* it is impossible to draw conclusions about onomastic congruence since no two persons share a common name and the only qualified names belong to public royal figures or military leaders.[246] In other words, there are no patterns of a "situation on the ground." *Life of Apollonius*, a composition on the verge of novel and βίος, and the *Alexander Romance* contain impressively complex naming patterns, although they are positively incongruous in several respects. Sometimes place names and personal names are conflated, historical figures are confused, and whole lists of names are completely unattested elsewhere.[247] *Alex.* 2.14.1 contains a list of eight members of Alexander the Great's court with names belonging to no historical persons throughout the age of Alexander; Krzysztof Nawotka comments, "there are most probably no historical characters referred to here."[248] *Vita Apoll.* 6.1–10 lists a cluster of apparently Egyptian persons, but the majority are consistently common in the LGPN and consistently rare in ProsPtol.[249]

Biographies

Surprisingly, many βίοι also lack onomastic congruence. Diogenes Laertius' *Life of Pythagoras*, for example, does not contain enough onomastic data to be determinative. With only twenty names, neither is the Gospel of John. *Agesilaus*, like John, contains entirely too few names (only twenty) to be determinative.

A lack of onomastic congruence, not only in the case of the Fourth Gospel and *Agesilaus*, but also in the case of double tradition and M material, cannot be used to render a negative verdict on their authenticity. A lack of determinative patterns in the Fourth Gospel and *Agesilaus*, for example, could result from the personal nature of these works (i.e., from a lack of a reliance on named sources); further, dependence on a tradition that is less narratively focused could lead to fewer names being incorporated. Certainty, the case against a composition's authenticity is increased when naming patterns are demonstrated to be positively incongruous (as with the apocryphal material discussed above), but the criterion of onomastic congruence only functions to be relevant for the compositions that contain it. In other words, onomastic congruence positively reflects a historiographical interest, but a lack of onomastic congruence does not disprove it.

Demonax recounts twenty-eight names and qualifies only seven; each qualified name is relatively popular and hence appropriate for qualification in a local setting, but beyond this no further patterns can be determined.[250] About half of the fifty persons in *Agricola* have single names, while the rest are listed by their nomen and cognomen together.[251] *Agricola* contains onomastic congruence on two layers, although somewhat superficially; first, single names are generally rarer than qualified names, which is a natural pattern; second, three of the two common names in *Agricola*—Julius (4x) and Caesar (2x)—are also commonly attested in the PIR; yet Nerva, attested twice in *Agricola*, is very uncommon.[252]

Josephus' *Vita* has strong onomastic congruence. It names over ninety Jewish persons (over one hundred persons in total), many of whom share common names: Simon (6x), Matthias (3x), Jonathan (4x), Joseph (2x), Julius (2x), Herod (4x), Agrippa (3x), John (2x), Jesus (6x), Levi (3x), Philip (2x), Ananias (2x), Justus (4x), Crispus (2x), Capellus (2x), and James (2x). Josephus qualifies all but approximately twenty names, most of which are comparatively rare and would need no qualification.[253] Furthermore, percentages of named persons coincide well with Ilan I; a random sampling of popular names in *Vita*, for instance—Simon, Matthias, Jonathan, and Jesus—amounts to 20.4% of named Jewish persons in *Vita* versus 16% in Ilan I.[254]

Plutarch's *Caesar* contains over one hundred and twenty named persons, over thirty qualified names, and it contains seven common names. If we focus on names in the DPRR from 110

BCE–40 BCE to create an onomastic snapshot, we discover that common names from the DPRR are typically qualified in *Caesar* and that percentages of common names loosely reflect the DPRR (especially for *nomina*, e.g., Cornelius—3.6% of named persons in *Caesar* versus 2.4% in the DPRR). Yet there are exceptions: Publius and Marcus, for example, amount to 1.6% and 2.4% of names in *Caesar*, respectively, while they account for 7.7% and 11.5% of *praenomina* in the DPRR.[255]

Suetonius' *Divus Julius*, like Josephus' *Vita*, contains strong onomastic congruence. It names more than a hundred and forty persons, qualifies more than one hundred names, and contains fifteen common names. The unqualified names are relatively rare, and distributions of common *nomina* and *cognomina*—even *praenomina*—all generally reflect percentages in the DPRR.[256] Plutarch's most ambitious and informative biography, *Pompey*, also contains the most extensive onomastic data and congruence from the sources surveyed. It names more than one hundred seventy persons (approximately twenty non-Roman), more than twenty-five qualified names, and contains six common names while containing several layers of reflective onomastic patterns.[257] In our survey of twenty-three sources, the only works that bear onomastic congruence, as noted in Chapter 2, are those which Craig Keener suggests mark the height of historical sensitivity for the genre of the Greco-Roman βίος, and, especially in Plutarch, the apex of this genre within the Early Empire when expectations of historical reliability were at their highest.[258] Onomastic congruence appears to be a byproduct, however unintentional, of the information-driven nature of these historiographical works.

APPENDIX B

Semitisms Unique to Luke–Acts †

Location	Nature of Content	Semitism
1.5 L		In those days + name (LXX)
1.6 L		πορεύεσθαι ἐν (LXX)
1.8–9 L		(καὶ) ἐγένετο (δέ)
1.10 L		Periphrastic imperfect
1.11 L		θυσιαστήριον (biblical)
1.15 L		ἐνώπιον w/genitive
1.17L		ἐνώπιον w/genitive Unstressed καὶ αυτός
1.19 L		ἐνώπιον w/genitive ἀποκριθεὶς/εἶσα εἶπεν
1.20 L		καὶ ἰδού
1.23 L		(καὶ) ἐγένετο (δέ)
1.32 L		Son of the Most High
1.39 L		ἀναστάς/ᾶσα/άντες with verb of movement καὶ ἰδού

---

†L = Special Luke; AM = "in addition to Mark" (material Luke used to supplement Mark's text); AMT = "in addition to Matthew" (material Luke used to supplement a text he shares with Matthew). Italicized text indicates uncertainty regarding the text's status as a Semitism. Underlined portions indicate concentrations of Semitic syntax or vocabulary, esp. around key Semitic discourse markers (καὶ) ἐγένετο (δέ) and καὶ ἰδού.

1.41 L		(καὶ) ἐγένετο (δέ)
1.42 L		Positive denoting comparative
		Lack of the copula εἰμί
1.43 L		Lack of the copula εἰμί
1.50 L		From generation to generation (LXX)
1.51 L		ποιεῖν κράτος (LXX)
1.59 L		(καὶ) ἐγένετο (δέ)
1.68 L		Lack of the copula εἰμί
1.69 L		To raise up a horn (non-LXX)
1.72 L		To perform mercy (LXX)
1.75 L		All the days of our lives (LXX)
		ἐνώπιον w/genitive
1.76 L		ἐνώπιον w/genitive
1.78 L		πλάγχνα ἐλέους (non-LXX)
2.1 L		In those days (LXX)
		(καὶ) ἐγένετο (δέ)
2.6 L		(καὶ) ἐγένετο (δέ)
2.8–9 L		Figura etymologica
2.14 L		ἀνθρώποις εὐδοκίας
2.15 L		(καὶ) ἐγένετο (δέ)
2.21 L		Parataxis
2.25 L		ἄνθρωπος
		καὶ ἰδού
2.28 L		Unstressed καὶ αυτός
		Parataxis
2.33 L		Periphrastic imperfect

2.41 L		πάσχα
2.46 L		(καὶ) ἐγένετο (δέ)
3.21 AM		(καὶ) ἐγένετο (δέ)
		ἐν τῷ + infinitive
3.23 L		Unstressed καὶ αυτός
4.2 AMT		In those days
4.7 AMT		ἐνώπιον w/genitive
4.8 AMT		ἀποκριθεὶς/εἶσα εἶπεν
4.10 AMT		τοῦ + infinitive
4.12 AMT		ἀποκριθεὶς/εἶσα εἶπεν
4.15 AM		Unstressed καὶ αυτός
4.20 AM		Periphrastic imperfect
4.24 AM		ἀμὴν λέγω ὑμῖν
4.25 AM		In those days + name
4.29 AM		ἀναστάς/ᾶσα/άντες with verb of movement
4.31 AM		Periphrastic imperfect
4.34 AM		Lack of the copula εἰμί
4.39 AM		ἀναστάς/ᾶσα/άντες with verb of movement
4.44 AM		Periphrastic imperfect
5.1–2a AM	Special material on Peter's call	Periphrastic imperfect
		Unstressed καὶ αυτός
		ἐν τῷ + infinitive
		Parataxis
		(καὶ) ἐγένετο (δέ)
5.5L		ἀποκριθεὶς/εἶσα εἶπεν
5.7 L		τοῦ + infinitive
		ἐρχόμενος/ἐλθών

5.12 AM	Extra material on healing of man with leprosy	(καὶ) ἐγένετο (δέ) ἐν τῷ + infinitive καὶ ἰδού Parataxis Lack of the copula εἰμί
5.14 AM		Unstressed καὶ αυτός
5.16 AM		Periphrastic imperfect
5.17 AM	Extra material on healing of paralytic	Periphrastic imperfect (καὶ) ἐγένετο (δέ) Unstressed καὶ αυτός Parataxis
5.18 AM		ἄνθρωπος ἐνώπιον w/genitive
5.22 AM		ἀποκριθεὶς/εῖσα εἶπεν
5.25 AM		ἐνώπιον w/genitive
5.29 AM		Periphrastic imperfect
5.31 AM		ἀποκριθεὶς/εῖσα εἶπεν
5.35 AM		In those days
5.39 AM		Positive denoting comparative
6.3 AM		ἀποκριθεὶς/εῖσα εἶπεν
6.6 AM		(καὶ) ἐγένετο (δέ)
6.12 AM		(καὶ) ἐγένετο (δέ) Periphrastic imperfect
6.20 AMT		Unstressed καὶ αυτός
6.22 AMT		Cast your name as evil Son of Man
6.34 AMT		Lack of the copula εἰμί
6.38 AMT		Third active plural denoting passive

6.48 AMT		ἄνθρωπος
6.49 AMT		ἄνθρωπος
7.3 AMT		ἐρχόμενος/ἐλθών
7.11–12 L	Special material on widow in Nain	(καὶ) ἐγένετο (δέ) καὶ ἰδού Parataxis
7.37 AM		καὶ ἰδού
7.39 L		Lack of the copula εἰμί
7.40 L		ἀποκριθεὶς/εἶσα εἶπεν
7.50 L		εἰρήνη as a greeting (LXX)
8.1 L	Special material with the list of women who served Jesus	Unstressed καὶ αυτός (καὶ) ἐγένετο (δέ) Parataxis
8.5 AM		Birds of the sky (Hebrew Bible)
8.22 AM		(καὶ) ἐγένετο (δέ)
8.40 AM		ἐν τῷ + infinitive
8:42 AM		ἐν τῷ + infinitive
8.47 AM		ἐνώπιον w/genitive
9.18 AM		(καὶ) ἐγένετο (δέ)
9.19 AM		ἀποκριθεὶς/εἶσα εἶπεν
9.28 AM	Extra Petrine material on transfiguration	(καὶ) ἐγένετο (δέ) After these things
9.29 AM		(καὶ) ἐγένετο (δέ) ἐν τῷ + infinitive
9.33 AM		(καὶ) ἐγένετο (δέ) ἐν τῷ + infinitive
9.34 AM		ἐν τῷ + infinitive
9.36 AM		In those days ἐν τῷ + infinitive

9.37 AM		(καὶ) ἐγένετο (δέ)
9.38 AM		ἀνήρ
		καὶ ἰδού
9.39 AM		καὶ ἰδού
		Parataxis
9.49 AM		ἀποκριθεὶς/εἶσα εἶπεν
9.51 L	Key verse on Jesus setting his face to Jerusalem	τοῦ + infinitive
		ἐν τῷ + infinitive
		(καὶ) ἐγένετο (δέ)
		Unstressed καὶ αυτός
		πρόσωπον (biblical)
9.52 L		ἀποστέλλειν πρὸ προσώπου with genitive
9.53 L		πρόσωπον
		Periphrastic imperfect
10.1 AMT		ἀποστέλλειν πρὸ προσώπου with genitive
10.5 AMT		εἰρήνη as a greeting
10.6 AMT		υἱός εἰρήνης
10.18 L		σατανᾶς
10.25 AM		καὶ ἰδού
10.27 AM		ἀποκριθεὶς/εἶσα εἶπεν
10.35 L		ἐν τῷ + infinitive
10.37 L		To perform mercy (LXX)
10.38 L		ἐν τῷ + infinitive
10.41 L		ἀποκριθεὶς/εἶσα εἶπεν
10.42 L		Positive denoting comparative
11.1 AMT		(καὶ) ἐγένετο (δέ)
		ἐν τῷ + infinitive

11.7 L		ἀποκριθεὶς/εἶσα εἶπεν
11.14 AMT		(καὶ) ἐγένετο (δέ)
		Periphrastic imperfect
11.27 L	Special comment from a woman in the crowd	(καὶ) ἐγένετο (δέ)
		ἐν τῷ + infinitive
11.37 AMT		ἐν τῷ + infinitive
11.41 AMT		καὶ ἰδού
11.45 AMT		ἀποκριθεὶς/εἶσα εἶπεν
11.46 AMT		Figura etymologica (non-LXX)
11.51 AMT		θυσιαστήριον (biblical)
12.6 AMT		ἐνώπιον w/genitive
12.8 AMT		Son of Man
12.9 AMT		ἐνώπιον w/genitive
12.10 AMT		To speak a word against (Aramaic)
12.19 L		ψυχή in a reflective sense
12.20 L		Third active plural denoting passive
12.37 L		ἀμήν λέγω υμῖν
		ἐρχόμενος/ἐλθών
12.48 L		Third active plural denoting passive
12.49 L		τί used as adverb denoting 'how' (Aramaic)
13.2 L		Positive denoting comparative
		ἀποκριθεὶς/εἶσα εἶπεν
13.7 L		ἰδού as particle for time
13.10		Periphrastic imperfect

13.11 L	Special material on healing of crippled woman	καὶ ἰδού Lack of copulative
13.14 L		ἀποκριθεὶς/εῖσα εἶπεν ἐρχόμενος/ἐλθών
13.16 L		σατανᾶς ἰδού as particle for time
13.23 AMT		Lack of the copula εἰμί
13.25 AMT		ἀποκριθεὶς/εῖσα εἶπεν Parataxis
13.26 AMT		ἐνώπιον w/genitive
13.30 L		καὶ ἰδού
13.32 L		πορευθείς/έντες (Aramaic)
14.1 L	Special material about Jesus in the house of a prominent pharisee	(καὶ) ἐγένετο (δέ) ἐν τῷ + infinitive πορευθείς/έντες Periphrastic imperfect Parataxis
14.2 L		καὶ ἰδού
14.3 L		ἀποκριθεὶς/εῖσα εἶπεν
14.9 L		ἐρχόμενος/ἐλθών
14.10 L		ἐνώπιον w/genitive
14.18 AMT		ἀπό μιᾶς
14.26 AMT		ψυχή in a reflective sense
14.35 AMT		Third active plural denoting passive
15.1 AM		Periphrastic imperfect
15.7 AMT		Positive denoting comparative
15.10 L		ἐνώπιον w/genitive

15.14 L		Unstressed καὶ αυτός
15.18 L		ἐνώπιον w/genitive
		ἀναστάς/ᾶσα/άντες with verb of movement
15.20 L		ἀναστάς/ᾶσα/άντες with verb of movement
15.25 L		ἐρχόμενος/ἐλθών
15.29 L		ἰδού as particle for time
		ἀποκριθεὶς/εἶσα εἶπεν
16.6 L		βάτος 'bath' (non-LXX)
16.7 L		κόρος 'measure'
16.8 L		Sons of this age
		Sons of light
		(τῆς) ἀδικίας
16.9 L		μαμωνᾶς (Aramaic)
		Third active plural denoting passive
16.15 L		ἐνώπιον w/genitive
16.21 L		ἐρχόμενος/ἐλθών
16.22 L		ἐγένετο (δέ)
16.24 L		Unstressed καὶ αυτός
17.1 AMT		τοῦ + infinitive
17.11 L	Jesus heals men with leprosy	(καὶ) ἐγένετο (δέ)
		ἐν τῷ + infinitive
		Parataxis
17.13 L		Unstressed καὶ αυτός
17.14 L		(καὶ) ἐγένετο (δέ)
		πορευθείς/έντες
17.17 L		ἀποκριθεὶς/εἶσα εἶπεν

17.19 L		ἀναστάς/ᾶσα/άντες with verb of movement
17.21 L		Lack of the copula εἰμί
17.22 AMT		Son of Man
17.23 AMT		Lack of the copula εἰμί
17.26 AMT		In those days + name
17.28 AMT		In those days + name
18.5 L		ἐρχόμενος/ἐλθών
18.6 L		(τῆς) ἀδικίας
18.8 L		Son of Man
18.12 L		σάββατον in the sense of 'week' ἀποδεκατῶ
18.14 L		Positive denoting comparative
18.35 AM	Extra material on Bartimaeus (in Jericho)	(καὶ) ἐγένετο (δέ) ἐν τῷ + infinitive
19.2 L	Special material on Zacchaeus (in Jericho)	καὶ ἰδού Unstressed καὶ αυτός (twice) Lack of the copula εἰμί
19.10 L		Son of Man
19.11 AMT	Parable given before Zacchaeus and crowd (in Jericho)	Adverbial προστίθημι (Lukan Semitism) (καὶ) ἐγένετο (δέ)
19.15 AMT		(καὶ) ἐγένετο (δέ) ἐν τῷ + infinitive Parataxis
19.29 L		(καὶ) ἐγένετο (δέ)
19.40 AM		ἀποκριθεὶς/εῖσα εἶπεν
19.47 AM		Periphrastic imperfect

20.1 L		(καὶ) ἐγένετο (δέ)
20.11 AM		Adverbial προστίθημι
20.21 AM		πρόσωπον
20.34 AM		Sons of this age
20.36 AM		Sons of resurrection
20.39 AM		ἀποκριθείς/εῖσα εἶπεν
21.22 AM		τοῦ + infinitive
21.35 AM		'Upon the face of...'
21.36 AM		Son of Man
21.37 AM		Periphrastic imperfect
22.6 AM		τοῦ + infinitive
22.8 AM		πορευθείς/έντες
22.15 L		πάσχα
22.31 L	Extra Petrine material	τοῦ + infinitive
		σατανᾶς
22.47 AM		Lack of the copula εἰμί
22.48 AM		Son of Man
23.1 AM		ἀναστάς/ᾶσα/άντες with verb of movement
23.2 AM		ἀποκριθείς/εῖσα εἶπεν
23.8 L		Periphrastic imperfect
23.14 L		καὶ ἰδού
23.15 L		ἐνώπιον w/genitive
23.40 AM		ἀποκριθείς/εῖσα εἶπεν
23.43 L		Truly I say to you
23.50 AM		καὶ ἰδού
		Lack of the copula εἰμί
24.4 AM	Women at the tomb	(καὶ) ἐγένετο (δέ)
		ἐν τῷ + infinitive
		Parataxis
24.7 AM		Son of Man

24.11 AM		ἐνώπιον w/genitive
24.12 AM		ἀναστάς/ᾶσα/άντες with verb of movement
24.13 L	Road to Emmaus	καὶ ἰδού Periphrastic imperfect
24.14 L		Unstressed καὶ αυτός
24.15 L		(καὶ) ἐγένετο (δέ) ἐν τῷ + infinitive
24.17 L		Lack of the copula εἰμί
24.18 L		ἀποκριθεὶς/εῖσα εῖπεν
24.29 L		τοῦ + infinitive
24.30 L		(καὶ) ἐγένετο (δέ)
24.36 L		εἰρήνη as a greeting (LXX)
24.43 L		ἐνώπιον w/genitive
24.45		τοῦ + infinitive
24.49 L		καὶ ἰδού
24.51 L		(καὶ) ἐγένετο (δέ)
Acts 1.3		Resumptive pronoun followed by relative clause
1.10		καὶ ἰδού Periphrastic imperfect
1.13		Periphrastic imperfect
1.14		Periphrastic imperfect
2.1		ἐν τῷ + infinitive
2.2		Periphrastic imperfect
2.25		ἐνώπιον w/genitive
2.42		Periphrastic imperfect
3.2		τοῦ +infinitive Third active plural denoting passive

3.13		κατά ἐνώπιον w/genitive
3.26		ἐν τῷ + infinitive
4.5	Petrine material	(καὶ) ἐγένετο (δέ)
		ἐγένετο (δέ)
4.10		ἐνώπιον w/genitive
4.19		ἐνώπιον w/genitive
		ἀποκριθεὶς/εἶσα εἶπεν
4.30		ἐν τῷ + infinitive
5.3	Petrine material	σατανᾶς
5.6		ἀναστάς/ᾶσα/άντες with verb of movement
5.7		(καὶ) ἐγένετο (δέ)
5.9		Lack of the copula εἰμί
5.28		καὶ ἰδού
		Figura etymologica
5.29		ἀποκριθεὶς/εἶσα εἶπεν
5.31		τοῦ + infinitive
6.5		ἐνώπιον w/genitive
6.6		ἐνώπιον w/genitive
6.11		To speak against (Aramaic)
7.19		τοῦ + infinitive
7.41		In those days
7.45		In those days + name
7.46		ἐνώπιον w/genitive
7.56		Son of Man
8.1		Periphrastic imperfect
8.6		ἐν τῷ + infinitive
8.24	Philip and Eunuch	ἀποκριθεὶς/εἶσα εἶπεν

8.27		καὶ ἰδού
		ἀναστάς/ᾶσα/άντες with verb of movement
8.28		Periphrastic imperfect
8.34		ἀποκριθεὶς/εῖσα εἶπεν
8.36		Lack of the copula εἰμί
9.3		ἐν τῷ + infinitive
9.9		Periphrastic imperfect
9.10		Lack of the copula εἰμί
9.11		ἀναστάς/ᾶσα/άντες with verb of movement
9.15		ἐνώπιον w/gen.
		τοῦ + infinitive
9.28		Periphrastic imperfect
9.32		ἐγένετο (δέ)
9.37		ἐγένετο (δέ)
		In those days
9.39		ἀναστάς/ᾶσα/άντες with verb of movement
9.43		ἐγένετο (δέ)
10.12		Birds of the sky (Hebrew Bible)
10.15		τοῦ + infinitive
10.19		Lack of the copula εἰμί
10.20		ἀναστάς/ᾶσα/άντες with verb of movement
10.23		ἀναστάς/ᾶσα/άντες with verb of movement
10.24		Periphrastic imperfect
10.28		ἄνθρωπος

10.30	Petrine material	Periphrastic imperfect
		καὶ ἰδού
		ἐνώπιον w/gen.
10.31		ἐνώπιον w/gen.
11.6		Birds of the sky (Hebrew Bible)
11.11		καὶ ἰδού
11.15		ἐν τῷ + infinitive
11.26		ἐγένετο (δέ)
12.3		Adverbial προστίθημι
12.4		πάσχα
		Resumptive pronoun followed by relative clause
12.5		Periphrastic imperfect
12.6		Periphrastic imperfect
12.7		καὶ ἰδού
12.12		Periphrastic imperfect
12.20		Periphrastic imperfect
13.6		Lack of the copula εἰμί
13.11		Lack of the copula εἰμί
13.24		ἀποστέλλειν πρὸ προσώπου with genitive
14.1		ἐγένετο (δέ)
14.7		Periphrastic imperfect
14.20		ἀναστάς/ᾶσα/άντες with verb of movement
15.20		τοῦ + infinitive
16.1		καὶ ἰδού
16.9		Periphrastic imperfect
16.16		ἐγένετο (δέ)
16.36		εἰρήνη as a greeting
18.7		Periphrastic imperfect

18.10		τοῦ + infinitive
19.1		ἐγένετο (δέ)
		ἐν τῷ + infinitive
19.4		Figura etymologicae
19.9		ἐνώπιον w/genitive
19.14		Periphrastic imperfect
19.15		ἀποκριθεὶς/εἶσα εἶπεν
19.19		ἐνώπιον w/genitive
20.3		τοῦ + infinitive
20.7		σάββατον
21.3		Periphrastic imperfect
21.12		τοῦ + infinitive
22.6		ἐγένετο (δέ)
22.10		ἀναστάς/ᾶσα/άντες with verb of movement
22.17–8		ἐγένετο (δέ)
22.19		Periphrastic imperfect
22.20		Periphrastic imperfect
23.14		Figura etymologicae
23.20		τοῦ + infinitive
25.9		ἀποκριθεὶς/εἶσα εἶπεν
26.18		σατανᾶς
		τοῦ + infinitive
27.1		τοῦ + infinitive
27.24		καὶ ἰδού
27.35		ἐνώπιον w/gen.
28.8		ἐγένετο (δέ)
28.17		ἐγένετο (δέ)

Endnotes

1 *The Historical Paul in Acts* (Milton Keynes: Paternoster, 2019).

2 Bella DePaulo et al., "Cues to Deception," *Psychological Bulletin* 129 (2003), pp. 74–118.

3 Ibid., p. 75.

4 Ibid., p. 93.

5 Ibid., p. 94.

6 Ibid., p. 96.

7 There is wide early attestation in support of the traditional authorship (Irenaeus, *Haer.* 3.1.1, 3.13.3; Clement of Alexandria, *Strom.* 5.12; P[75]), but I do not assume it for our arguments here and use the name "Luke" as a mere shorthand for the author of Luke-Acts, as I do with the other Gospel authors. For further study on the authorship of the Gospels, I highly recommend the article by Simon Gathercole, "The Alleged Anonymity of the Canonical Gospels," *JTS* 69.2 (October 2018), pp. 447–476.

8 Text is THGNT.

9 Author's translation.

10 John Peters, "Luke's Source Claims in the Context of Ancient Historiography," *JSHJ* 18.1 (2020), pp. 35–60, and *Luke Among the Ancient Historians* (Eugene, OR: Pickwick, 2022).

11 Luke's "craft terminology" is discussed by Peters, *Luke Among the Ancient Historians*, p. 225. The closest linguistic parallel to the cluster of Luke's word choices in his preface comes from Demosthenes (*Against Olympiodorus* 48.40), according to a TLG search. In this instance, Demosthenes has crafted a legal speech on behalf of Olympiodorus' brother-

in-law, Callistratus. Callistratus' claims are that he and Olympiodorus had agreed to split the estate of a certain man from Halae named Comon and that Olympiodorus had failed to live up to this agreement. Demosthenes' point to the jury is that Olympiodorus refuses to let those "in the know" speak to the issue. Why does he refuse to allow them to speak? Because Olympiodorus knows that they were in a position to falsify his claims. In this context, παρηκολουθηκόσιν ἐξ ἀρχῆς ("having followed [everything] from the beginning"; cf. Luke 1.3) refers to the enduring inside perspective held by these relatives, giving them the unique position to judge all things accurately (ἀκριβῶς ἅπαντα ταῦτα τὰ πράγματα). Almost every key word in this text is also used by Luke in his prologue to legitimate his writing project.

12 See Loveday Alexander, *The Preface to Luke's Gospel: Literary Convention and Social Context in Luke 1.1–4 and Acts 1.1* (SNTSMS; Cambridge: Cambridge University Press, 1993), p. 33. Alexander's thesis is that Luke's preface has more in common with scientific treatises; for a response, see Sean Adams, "Luke's Preface (1.1–4) and its Relationship to Greek Historical Prefaces: A Response to Loveday Alexander," *JGRChJ* 3 (2006), pp. 170–191. For another discussion on the historiographical qualities of Luke's preface, see Clare K. Rothschild, *Luke-Acts and the Rhetoric of History: An Investigation of Early Christian Historiography* (WUNT 175; Tübingen: Mohr Siebeck, 2004), pp. 67–69.

13 Samuel Byrskog, *Story as History, History as Story: The Gospel Tradition in the Context of Ancient Oral History* (Tübingen: Mohr Siebeck: 2000), pp. 58–59, 251–252; Guido Schepens, "Traveling Greek Historians," in Maria Gabriella Bertinelli Angeli and Angela Donati (eds.), *Le vie della storia* (Rome: Bretschneider, 2006), pp. 81–102.

14 Guido Schepens remarks: "No doubt, the main reason for undertaking extended travels was for Herodotus to get in touch with as many sources as possible and to verify information by cross-checking. Even where information is sketchy, he wishes to learn what can be known on the basis of the available evidence. Thus his curiosity about the nature of Heracles led him to sail to Tyre and Thasos (2.44, cf. 2.102), 'as though there were nothing remarkable in making such a lengthy journey for the sake of researching a single point' (Romm 1998: 51–52)" ("History and *Historia*: Inquiry in the Greek Historians," in John Marincola (ed.),

A Companion to Greek and Roman Historiography (Oxford: Blackwell, 2007), p. 45).

15 Alexander, *The Preface*, p. 33; Peters, "Luke's Source Claims," p. 38.

16 John Marincola, *Authority and Tradition in Ancient Historiography* (Cambridge: Cambridge University Press, 1997), pp. 78–81, esp. 79; Marincola also comments, on p. 78, "the Roman recognition of the value of inquiry is suggested by A. Hirtius who, in the preface of Book VIII of the *Gallic War* of Caesar, apologizes for daring the complete Caesar's work, since Hirtius was not present at the events."

17 An interest in living eyewitnesses is also supported by Papias of Hierapolis (ca. 100 CE) when he comments that he preferred to consult "the living and abiding voice" (ζώσης φωνῆς καὶ μενούσης) as opposed to books when it came to gaining knowledge about Jesus. In context, Papias mentions several apostles by name as well as their disciples, and we are left to assume that he consulted these followers of the apostles directly about the apostles' experiences (see Eusebius, *Hist. Eccl.* 3.39.1). Eusebius illustrates this practice of Papias elsewhere (*Hist. Eccl.* 3.39.9) when commenting that Papias received accounts directly from Philip's daughters as well as from Justus Barsabbas, all individuals mentioned in Acts (1.23, 6.5, 21.8–9). Ecclesiastical traditions are likewise widespread in stressing Luke's proximity to the apostles, emphasizing that Luke was a follower of not only Paul but also, as Irenaeus states, "a follower and disciple of the apostles" (*Haer.* 3.10.1). Eusebius, indeed, interprets the Lukan prologue to say, not that Luke followed all *things* closely for a long time but rather that Luke followed all *the eyewitnesses and ministers of the word* for a long time (*Hist. Eccl.* 3.4.7), and this seems to be the reading of Luke 1.3 that Irenaeus assumes. It is not the most natural reading, however, since πάντα [πᾶσιν] lacks the article (See David Moessner, "Luke as Tradent and Hermeneut: "As one who has a thoroughly informed familiarity with all the events from the top" (παρηκολουθηκότι ἄνωθεν πᾶσιν ἀκριβῶς, Luke 1.3)," *NovTest* 58.3 (2016) pp. 259–300, esp. 292, n. 39.

18 For a discussion of how corroborative evidence functions in a case, see David Godden, "Corroborative Evidence," in C. Reed and C.W. Tindale (eds), *Dialectics, Dialogue and Argumentation: An Examination of Douglas Walton's Theories of Reasoning and Argument* (London: College Publications, 2014), pp. 201–212.

19 See Godden, "Corroborative Evidence," pp. 203–205.

20 See Peters, *Luke Among the Ancient Historians*, pp. 97–101, 205.

21 This brief discussion is based on Richard Fellows, "Mariam became Maria and, with that name, was Luke's source for the infancy narrative," a Jan. 5, 2021, post on his blog, *Paul and Co-workers*. URL retrieved on Dec. 26, 2021: http://paulandco-workers.blogspot.com/2021/01/mariam-be-came-maria-and-with-that-name.html. Fellows considers the available data across the spectrum of manuscript traditions when discussing his conclusions. The Semitic form Μαριάμ is indeclinable, although the de-clinable form of Μαρία in the first declension genitive acts as a supple-tive and is also considered by Fellows to be Semitic; cf. Peter Williams, 'Christmas Variants (3)', *Evangelical Textual Criticism* (http://evangelical-textualcriticism.blogspot.com/2005/12/christmas-variants-3.html; URL from this blog post retrieved on February 14, 2022).

22 Darrell Bock, *Luke*, Vol. 2 (BECNT; Grand Rapids, Michigan: 1996), p. 6.

23 Biblical quotations in this book, unless otherwise noted, are NIV.

24 For the case in favor of received written traditions, see: Chang-Wook Jung, *The Original Language of the Lukan Infancy Narrative*, JSNTSup, 267. (London: T&T Clark International, 2004); Stephen Farris, *The Hymns of Luke's Infancy Narratives: Their Origin, Meaning and Signifi-cance* (London: Bloomsbury Academic, 1985), pp. 31–66; Ben F. Meyer, "'But Mary Kept All These Things…' (Lk 2, 19.51)," *CBQ* 26.1 (1964), pp. 31–49, esp. 49. That Luke 1–2 in its entirety was composed without written source materials cannot be disproven.

25 Richard Bauckham is not convinced that Mary could have been a personal source for Luke given her age and the time at which Luke could have met her, but he believes James, the brother of Jesus, is a possible source. See his discussion in "Luke's Infancy Narrative as Oral History in Scriptural Form," in *The Gospels: History and Christology: The Search of Joseph Ratzinger-Benedict XVI*, ed. Bernardo Estrada, Erme-negildo Manicardi and Armand Puig i Tàrrech, Vol. 1 (Vatican City: Libreria Editrice Vaticana, 2013), pp. 399–417.

26 Yardenna Alexandre, "The Settlement History of Nazareth in the Iron Age and Early Roman Period," *'Atiqot* 98 (2020), pp. 25–92.

27 Cf. Alexandre, "Settlement History," pp. 27, 80.

28 My thanks to Dr. Alexandre for her gracious correspondence; for a visual of Old Nazareth, see the lithograph from David Robert's *The Holy Land, Syria, Idumea, Arabia, Egypt and Nubia* (London, 1855) as reprinted in Yardenna Alexandre, "Yafi'a," *HA–ESI* 124 (October 3, 2012), Fig. 8.3.

29 Tell 3 arguably provides an exception.

30 On the problem of miracles, see: Michael Licona, *The Resurrection of Jesus: A New Historiographical Approach* (Downers Grove: IVP Academic, November 2010); Craig Keener, *Miracles: The Credibility of the New Testament Accounts* (2 Vols; Grand Rapids: Baker Academic, 2011). For a refutation of the most significant historical difficulties of Acts, namely the apparent disjunction between the Lukan Paul and the Pauline letters, see: Craig Keener, *Acts: An Exegetical Commentary* (4 Vols.; Grand Rapids, MI: Baker Academic, 2015), Vol. 1, pp. 231–233; Chae, *The Historical Paul*. For a recent discussion on the greatest historical problem in the Gospel of Luke, namely the census of Luke 2.1, see: David Armitage, "Detaching the Census: An Alternative Reading of Luke 2.1–7," *TynBul* 69.1 (2018), pp. 75–95; for a slightly less conservative perspective, see Mark Smith, "Of Jesus and Quirinius," *CBQ* 62 (2002), pp. 278–293; see also John H. Rhoads, "Josephus Misdated the Census of Quirinius," *JETS* 54 (2011), pp. 65–87; Edward Dabrowa, "The Date of the Census of Quirinius and the Chronology of the Governors of the Province of Syria," *ZPE* 178 (2011), pp. 137–142; Michael Wolter, "'Wann wurde Maria schwanger?' Eine vernachlässigte Frage und ihre Bedeutung für das Verständnis der lukanischen Vorgeschichte (Lk 1–2)," in *Von Jesus zum Christus: Christologische Studien*. Festgabe für. Paul Hoffmann zum 65. Geburtstag (BZNW 93; ed. by R. Hoppe and U. Busse; Berlin: Walter de Gruyter, 1998), pp. 405–422.

31 Andy Young et al., "The Faces That Launched a Thousand Slips: Everyday Difficulties and Errors in Recognizing People," *British Journal of Psychology* 76 (1985), pp. 495–523; Geoffrey Cohen, "Why is it Difficult to Put Names to Faces?," *British Journal of Psychology* 81 (1990), pp. 287–297; N. Stanhope and Geoffrey Cohen, "Retrieval of Proper Names: Testing the Modes," *British Journal of Psychology* 84 (1993), pp. 51–65; Geoffrey Cohen and Deborah Burke, "Memory for Proper

Names: A Review," *Memory* 1.4 (1993), pp. 249–263. Accounts of extraordinary ancient memories often focus on names: e.g. Plato repeating 50 names after hearing them once (*Hi. Maior* 285e), Seneca the Elder's claim of recalling 2000 names read to him in his youth (*Contr.* 1 pref. 2).

32 Deborah Burke et al., "On the Tip-of-the-tongue: What Causes Word Finding Failures in Young and Older Adults?," *Journal of Memory and Language* 30 (1991), pp. 542–579.

33 Young et al., "Slips"; Cohen and Burke, "Memory," p. 250.

34 Cohen, "Names," p. 288; Stanhope and Cohen, "Retrieval."

35 Judith Redman, "How Accurate Are Eyewitnesses? Bauckham and the Eyewitnesses in the Light of Psychological Research," *JBL* 129.1 (2010), pp. 177–197; Robert McIver, "Eyewitnesses as Guarantors of the Accuracy of the Gospel Traditions in the Light of Psychological Research," *JBL* 131.3 (2012), pp. 529–546; Dale Allison, *Constructing Jesus: Memory, Imagination, and History* (Grand Rapids: Baker Academic, 2010), pp. 1–30; Cohen, "Names," p. 289.

36 See Luuk Van de Weghe, "The Cerebral Scars of Shipwreck," *TynBul* 70.2 (2019), pp. 205–220, esp. 206–208.

37 Maria Assunta et al., "The Witnesses of Civitella," *Cardozo Studies in Law and Literature* 3.2 (1991), pp. 171–195; from a word count of approximately 12,300, only twenty-three persons are named while eighty-one are anonymous.

38 Renate Volbert, "Aussagen über traumatische Erlebnisse," *Forens Psychiatr Psychol Kriminol* 5 (2011), pp. 18–31; Willem Wagenaar and Jaap Groeneweg, "The Memory of Concentration Camp Survivors," *Applied Cognitive Psychology* 4 (1990), pp. 77–87.

39 Travis Derico, *Oral Tradition and Synoptic Verbal Agreement: Evaluating the Empirical Evidence for Literary Dependence* (Eugene, OR: Pickwick Publications, 2016), pp. 267–290. Derico provides transcripts from three interviews conducted in 2002–2003; his subjects are disciples of Roy Whitman, founder of a small Jordanian evangelical community in the late 1920s. The first transcript recounts fourteen names (885 words total); the second, four names (2000 words); the third, eight names (1900 words).

40 Richard Bauckham, "The Eyewitnesses and the Gospel Traditions," *JSHJ* 1.1 (2003), pp. 28–60, esp. 60; Bauckham, *Jesus and the Eyewitnesses*, p. 67; Simon Hornblower, "Personal Names and the Study of the Ancient Greek Historians," in *Greek Personal Names: Their Value as Evidence* (ed. Simon Hornblower and Elaine Matthew; Oxford: Oxford University Press, 2000), p. 131.

41 E.g., 15.6 percent of males are named Joseph and Simon in general; 18.2 percent of males are named Joseph and Simon in the Gospels and Acts (Bauckham, *Jesus and the Eyewitnesses*, pp. 71–75, 84; Tal Ilan, *Lexicon of Jewish Names in Late Antiquity: Part 1: Palestine 330 BCE—200 CE* (TSAJ, 91; Tübingen: Mohr Siebeck, 2002)).

42 In my 2022 PhD Dissertation (University of Aberdeen) as well as in my article, "Name Recall in the Synoptic Gospels," I address the problem that Ilan I does not provide an onomastic snapshot of Jesus' Palestine, since her database covers approximately five hundred years. This seems too broad to determine onomastic patterns. I refine Ilan's database to the years 30 BCE to 90 CE and confirm that onomastic congruence can still be demonstrated. Incidentally, Richard Bauckham is currently working on a new prosopography (50 BCE to 135 CE) with the aim of acquiring greater accuracy, correcting further errors discovered in Ilan I, and supplementing her data with new inscriptions being published by the *Corpus Inscriptionum Iudaeae/Palaestinae*. My thanks to Dr. Bauckham for providing his unpublished material for me to review; it is apparent that the efforts of acquiring more precise data will lead toward the further justification of onomastic congruence in the Gospels and Acts.

43 Michael Strickland, "What's in a Name? Richard Bauckham, First-Century Palestinian Jewish Names, and the Protoevangelium of James," *ATI* 7 (2014), pp. 35–42. Strickland argues that, like the Gospels-Acts, the *Protevangelium of James* contains first century Jewish Palestinian names without being authentic, yet he fails to appreciate relative distribution and the qualification of popular names.

44 This latter suggestion—that of informants' names embedded within certain accounts—has garnered significant criticism against Bauckham's thesis. See Christopher Tuckett, "Review of Richard Bauckham, Jesus and the Eyewitnesses," *RBL* 12 (2007); Samuel Byrskog, "The Eyewitnesses as Interpreters of the Past: Reflections on Richard

Bauckham's *Jesus and the Eyewitnesses*," *JSHS* 6.2 (2008), pp. 157–168, esp. 157; Stephen Patterson, "Can You Trust a Gospel? A Review of Richard Bauckham's Jesus and the Eyewitnesses," *JSHJ* 6.2 (2008), pp. 194–210, esp. 198–199; Craig Keener, "Review of Richard Bauckham, *Jesus and the Eyewitnesses*," *BBR* 19.1 (2009), pp. 130–132. Richard Bauckham has responded, however, by citing Simon Hornblower and giving an illustration from Plutarch's *Caesar* ("In Response to My Respondents: Jesus and the Eyewitnesses in Review," *JSHS* 6.2 (2008), pp. 225–253, esp. 226–228). Although I was particularly skeptical of this aspect of his argument and commenced this project with every intention of demonstrating that aspect to be unprovable, several lines of evidence—all addressed in the following chapters and Appendix A—moved me to accept it as plausible.

45 Typically, one needs around forty names to determine patterns that can be compared with data from prosopographies, and ideally some of these names will involve qualifiers; beyond this, several other factors impact the ability to draw comparisons. Greek names, for example, are much more variant than Roman and especially Jewish names, resulting in the case that one needs fewer names to determine patterns for the latter; on the other hand, more detail about naming trends is often available through volumes of the *LGPN*, which can influence the ability to draw comparisons favorably in the case of Greek names from certain provinces.

46 This point can be overemphasized, since Jewish persons bearing this theophoric name are attested in Palestine, albeit rarely and after 70 CE (e.g. Ilan I, p. 281; CIIP III 2179; CIIP IV 3484).

47 Σήμης, Δαθανς, Νεφθαλείμ, 1.1; Αντώνιος, Αστέριος, Αμνής, 2.4

48 Ilan I, pp. 432–433.

49 Onomastic congruence does not equal onomastic inerrancy, but it refers to a general pattern of corroboration. Cf. Tal Ilan and Jonathan Price, "Seven Onomastic Problems in Josephus' 'Bellum Judaicum'," *The Jewish Quarterly Review*, 84.2/3 (1993), pp. 189–208.

50 Craig Keener, *Christobiography: Memory, History, and the Reliability of the Gospels* (Grand Rapids: Eerdmans, 2019), pp. 15–18, 33–34, 68, 79–94, 150.

51 Williams, *Can We Trust the Gospels?*, Kindle edition.

52 Ibid.

53 This last observation appears quite arbitrary. Why consider the top nine names? Would choosing another arbitrary number produce less compelling results? Another concern is that Bauckham's math does not seem to be correct. The top nine names, according to his own tally of Ilan's numbers (See *Jesus and the Eyewitnesses*, p. 84), belong to a total of 1227 males (Simon, 243; Joseph, 218; Eleazar, 166; Judah, 164; Yohanan, 122; Joshua, 99; Hananiah, 82; Jonathan, 71; Mattathias, 62 = 1227). Bauckham himself notes, at the bottom of this very table, that the total number of named males counted by Ilan is 2625. But 1227 is not 41.5% of 2625; it is 46.7%. That these same nine names are held by thirty-two Jewish males in the Gospels and Acts, which amounts to 40.5% of persons (contra Bauckham's 40.3%), now seems slightly less impressive. But none of this compromises his main point. In fact, let us now take a different arbitrary number: the top six. According to Bauckham's rendering of Ilan I, 1012 males bear these six names: 38.6%. What percentage of males in the Gospels and Acts bear these same names? 34.2% (twenty-seven males), which is quite proximate.

54 Bauckham, *Jesus and the Eyewitnesses*, p. 42.

55 Mark Goodacre, *The Synoptic Problem: A Way Through the Maze* (New York: T & T Clark International, 2002), pp. 56–83. I do not take a firm position between the Farrer Hypothesis and the Two-Source Theory. When referring to "Q" I merely indicate the material shared by Luke and Matthew without implying that Luke's source for this material was the Gospel of Matthew or whether it was an additional, hitherto undiscovered, written source. A mixture of written and oral tradition in Q cannot be discounted as a further possibility; see James Dunn, "Altering the Default Setting: Re-envisaging the Early Transmission of the Jesus Tradition," *NTS* 49.2 (2003), 139–175; James Dunn, *Jesus Remembered* (Grand Rapids: Eerdmans, 2003), Ch. 8.

56 Ilan I, p. 18.

57 This is especially true for the Gospel of Luke. For the most thorough treatment to date, see Hogeterp and Denaux, *Semitisms in Luke's Greek*. For fuller discussion, see Chapter 6.

58 James Edwards, *The Hebrew Gospel and the Development of the Synoptic Tradition* (Grand Rapids: Eerdmans, 2009), pp. 141–145. Again, Edwards is not without his detractors (e.g. Mark Goodacre's review in *CBQ* 73.4 (2011), pp. 862–863).

59 Edwards, *Development*, pp. 145–147.

60 This section implicitly leans on criteria from C. Behan McCullagh, *Justifying Historical Descriptions* (Cambridge: Cambridge University Press, 1984), pp. 19–20.

61 For Gospels as memoirs: Clement of Alexandria, *Exc.* 1.20; Eusebius, *Eccl. Hist.* 2.15; Justin Martyr, *Dial.* 100.4, 101.3, 103.6; Irenaeus, *Haer.* 3.1.1.

62 Michael Licona, "Are the Gospels 'Historically Reliable'? A Focused Comparison of Suetonius's Life of Augustus and the Gospel of Mark," *Religions* 10 (2019), p. 148; Christopher Pelling, "Plutarch's Method of Work in the Roman Lives," *JHS* 99 (1979), pp. 74–96, esp. 87–90.

63 David Moessner, "Luke as Tradent and Hermeneut," pp. 292–293; Keener, *Christobiography*, pp. 87–88.

64 For a list of differences and possible uses of literary devices, see Michael Licona, *Why Are There Differences in the Gospels?* (New York: Oxford University Press, 2016). Licona's thesis concerning compositional devices has been thoroughly critiqued in Lydia McGrew's *The Mirror or the Mask: Liberating the Gospels from Literary Devices* (Chillicothe, Ohio: DeWard Publishing Company, 2019), to which Licona has responded in a lengthy blog post titled "Lydia McGrew Answered," available on his web page (https://www.risenjesus.com/lydia-mcgrew-answered). I find some of McGrew's criticisms helpful and insightful, but I also find the presence of literary creativity in the Gospels almost undeniable—not merely because these might account for alleged discrepancies, but because they occur, like Luke's historical tells, in discernable patterns within each Gospel. Any further engagement would go beyond the scope of our interests but suffice it to say—and this will become increasingly apparent in later chapters of the book—that I have sympathies with both perspectives.

65 Scot McKnight, "Jesus and the Twelve," *BBR* 11.2 (2001), pp. 203–231, esp. 203.

66 For their fading role and the discrepancy between Thaddaeus and Judas son of James, see: Dietrich-Alex Koch, "The Origin, Function and Disappearance of the 'Twelve': Continuity from Jesus to the Post-Easter Community?," *HTS* 61.1/2 (2005), pp. 211–229; McKnight, "Jesus and the Twelve," pp. 207–210; Bauckham, *Jesus and the Eyewitnesses*, pp. 93–108.

67 Carolyn Osiek, "The Women at the Tomb: What are They Doing There?," *HTS* 53.1/2 (1997), pp. 103–118.

68 Lydia McGrew, following James Blunt, terms these connections "undesigned coincidences." For her discussion of these, see p. 18 of her intriguing book, *Hidden in Plain View: Undesigned Coincidences in the Gospels and Acts*, (Chillicothe, Ohio: DeWard, 2017).

69 See Samuel Byrskog's discussion on Mark and Acts 10.34–43, *Story*, pp. 286–287; Richard Horsley, "Oral and Written Aspects in the Emergence of the Gospels of Mark as Scripture," *Oral Tradition* 25.1 (2010), pp. 93–114; Matthew Larsen, "Accidental Publication, Unfinished Texts and the Traditional Goals of New Testament Criticism," *JSNT* 39.4 (2017), pp. 362–387.

70 Kenneth Bailey, "Informal Controlled Oral Tradition," *Themelios* 20 (1995), pp. 4–11, esp. 7–8; Theodore Weeden, "Kenneth Bailey's Theory of Oral Tradition: A Theory Contested by Its Evidence," *JSHJ* 7.1 (2009), pp. 3–43; James Dunn, "Kenneth Bailey's Theory of Oral Tradition: Critiquing Theodore Weeden's Critique," *JSHJ* 7.1 (2009), pp. 44–62.

71 Rainer Riesner, *Jesus als Lehrer. Frühjüdische Volksbildung und Evangelien-Überlieferung*, WUNT 504 (Tübingen: Mohr Siebeck, 42023). See also Birger Gerhardsson, *The Reliability of the Gospel Tradition* (Grand Rapids: Baker Academic, 2001).

72 On which possible names, see Byrskog, *Story*, pp. 266–306; Bauckham, *Jesus and the Eyewitnesses*, pp. 524–535. Thucydides and Herodotus' works also contain prime examples of implicit eyewitness/informant allusions in name-dense portions of texts; see: Hornblower, *Personal Names*, pp. 139–140; R. Shroud, "Thucydides and Corinth," *Chiron* 24 (1994), pp. 267–302; cf. Byrskog, *Story*, pp. 49–91; Peters, "Source Claims," pp. 45–60; John Moles, "Luke's Preface: The Greek Decree,

Classical Historiography and Christian Redefinitions," *NTS* 57.4 (2011), pp. 461–482, esp. 479.

73 David Gill, "Dionysios and Damaris: A Note on Acts 17.34," *CBQ* 61.3 (1999), pp. 483–490.

74 Gill writes, "there is no reason to believe Luke did *not* invent the name [emphasis his]" ("Dionysios and Damaris," p. 487), although Damaris is attested twice elsewhere (LPGN V3a-9097, V1-52829).

75 Sterling Dow, "Lakhares, a Rare Athenian Name," *Classical Philology* 52.2 (1957), pp. 106–107. Another name in Acts 16–28, Ἔραστος, is uncommon but not rare (44 attestations in LGPN 1–5); others are more typical Greek names. Statistics on Greek names in Acts: Τιμόθεος (435 occurrences in LGPN I-V); Λυδία (6); Ἰάσων (738, although the spelling Ἰάσονος is unique); Διονύσιος (4762); Ἀκύλας (60); Σωσθένης (108); Ἔραστος (44), Δημήτριος (3325), Γάϊος (547), Ἀρίσταρχος (419), Ἀλέξανδρος (2359), Σώπατρος (235), Σεκοῦνδος (190), Τυχικός (97), Τρόφιμος (384), Εὔτυχος (551), Μνάσων (129), and Τρόφιμος (384).

76 Statistics from LGPN V5a, xvi: 51,293 total attestations, 4386 names singly attested; from LGPN V5b, xxx–xxxii: 44,748 total attestations, 4,775 names singly attested.

77 I prefer "qualified" to "disambiguated" since names are not necessarily qualified for the purpose of disambiguation; for this reason, it is the least reliable criterion for assessing onomastic congruence; nevertheless, even Simon Hornblower deems a high concentration of appropriate patronymics relevant to the discussion of eyewitness source material (*Personal Names*, p. 140), and see the discussion in Appendix A on onomastic patterns in Suetonius' *Divus Julius*.

78 E.g., LGPN 5b, Table 1.

79 A portion of this chapter is an extract from my article, "The Cerebral Scars of Shipwreck," *TynBul* 70.2 (2019), pp. 205–220.

80 Troy Troftgruben, "Slow Sailing in Acts: Suspense in the Final Sea Journey (Acts 27.1–28.15)," *JBL* 136.4 (2017), pp. 949–968, esp. 949. Troftgruben argues for a literary motive behind this length after a comparison of other ancient historiographers. I find his conclusion

questionable due to Luke's lack of historiographical literary style else-where in Luke-Acts.

81 Marius Reiser says, "Der Überblick über antike Seefahrt—und Schiffbrucherzählungen laßt schnell einen schlichten Befund erkennen: Es gibt keine wirkliche Parallele zu Act 27. In diesem Kapitel liegt uns der bei weitem genaueste und umfangreichste Bericht über eine Seereise aus der Antike vor (Marius Reiser, "Von Caesarea nach Malta: literarischer Charakter und historische Glaubwürdigkeit von Act 27," *Ende des Paulus: historische, theologische und literaturgeschichtliche Aspekte* [Berlin: Walter deGruyter, 2001], p. 51)." For a classic historical treatment of Lucian's shipwreck of the Isis, see: Lionel Casson, "The Isis and Her Voyage," *Transactions and Proceedings of the American Philological Association* 81 (1950), pp. 43–56; for a skeptical assessment of Lucian's historical interest, see: Graham Anderson, "Some Notes on Lucian's *Navigium*," *Mnemosyne* 30.4 (1977), pp. 363–368.

82 Colin J. Hemer, *The Book of Acts in the Setting of Hellenistic History* (ed. Conrad H. Gempf; Winona Lake, IN: Eisenbrauns, 1990), p. 389.

83 For nautical *hapax legomena*, see my discussion in "Cerebral Scars." For references to hope/survival, see Acts 27.20, 22, 31, 34, 43; 28.1, 4. Place names in Acts 27.1–28.15 include: Appii Forum (28.15), Clauda (27.16), Cnidus (27.7), Crete (27.7), Cyprus (27.4), Lasea (27.8), Lycia (27.5), Melita (28.1), Myra (27.5), Puteoli (28.13), Rhegium (28.13), Salmone (27.8), Sidon (27.3), Syracuse (28.12), Fair Havens (27.8), and Three Taverns (28.15).

84 John Gilchrist, "The Historicity of Paul's Shipwreck," *JSNT* 61 (March 1996), pp. 29–51, esp. p. 37.

85 Ibid., yet Gilchrist fails to highlight the substantial greatness of detail/length of Acts 27.1–28.15 even in comparison to the other "we" sections; As noted by Troftgruben, "A few days of story time correspond to multiple verses of text (27.1–4, 5–8, 9–12, 13–20, 27–32, etc.; cf. 20.13–17; 21.1–6) … Prior journey narratives occasionally approach this pace (14.22–23; 18.19–21; 21.4–6, 8–14) but not in so regular and sustained a fashion" ("Slow Sailing in Acts," p. 964).

86 See: Lionel Casson, "Speed under Sail of Ancient Ships," *Transactions of the American Philological Association* 82 (1951), pp. 136–148;

James Smith, *The Voyage and Shipwreck of St. Paul* (London: Longmans, Green and Co., 1856), pp. 95–124; R. W. White, "A meteorological appraisal of Acts 27.5–26," *The Expository Times* 113.12 (September 2002), pp. 403–407. Luke significantly notes that *the wind* drives them to the South of Crete (βραδυπλοοῦντες καὶ μόλις, γενόμενοι κατὰ τὴν Κνίδον, μὴ προσεῶντος ημᾶς τοῦ ανέμου, 27.6–7); this is a detail even William Ramsay overlooks ("Roads and Travel," *Hasting's Dictionary of the Bible*, Extra Volume (Edinburgh 2004), pp. 375–402); he attributes the southern sailing route alongside Crete to a lack of harbors on the northern coast (380), but Casson's study undermines Ramsay's claim and reveals him to be an exemplar of the kind of "armchair navigation" Luke's recollection avoids (Casson, "The Isis and Her Voyage," n. 16).

87 A prime example is the location of Cauda, an island approximately twenty miles South from the West of Crete (referred to in various MSS in Acts 27.6 as Καῦδα or Κλαῦδα). Luke notes its location accurately, confirmed by two early fragments (*I. Cret.* 2.7.1, p. 92—third century BCE.; *I. Cret.* 4.184—second century BCE); Pliny places it too close to the Western end of Crete (Plin. *NH* 4.12.62), while Ptolemy places its location some ninety miles East (Ptol. *Geog.* 3.17.1). For further detail, see: Colin J. Hemer, "First Person Narrative in Acts 27–28," *TynBul* 36 (1985), pp. 79–109, esp. 99.

88 An African twelve-point wind-rose bears the term εὐρακύλων in Latin only, 30 degrees N of E; σκάφη in its context is a likely transliteration from the Latin *scapha* (cf. Caes. *B.G.* 4.26.4), although later Greek usage in Plutarch and Strabo, etc., shows a preference for ἐφολχυς or ἐφολκυον (see Hemer, "First Person Narrative," pp. 98, 100; Reiser, "Von Caesarea nach Malta," p. 64).

89 Hemer, "First Person Narrative," p. 105.

90 Hemer, "First Person Narrative," p. 93.

91 Smith, *The Voyage and Shipwreck of St. Paul*, pp. 120–124. This location is not beyond dispute, but Smith and Hemer argue convincingly that navigational, literary, and geographical factors weigh in its favor (A. Acworth, "Where Was Paul Shipwrecked? A Re-examination of the Evidence," *JTS* 24.1 (April 1973), pp. 190–193; Colin J. Hemer, "Euraquilo and Melita," *JTS* 26.1 (1975), pp. 100–111.

154 | The Historical Tell

92 David Bird, "Pliny's Arrugia: Water Power in Roman Gold-mining," *Mining History* 15.4 (2004), pp. 59–60.

93 Gary Wells et al., "From the Lab to the Police Station: A Successful Application of Eyewitness Research," *American Psychol.* 55 (2000), p. 581, note that more than two thousand articles had been devoted to the study of eyewitness recollection by the turn of the millennium.

94 Trenary, "State," 1274–1280.

95 Trenary, "State," 1264–1274; Julie Shaw, *The Memory Illusion: Remembering, Forgetting, and the Science of False Memories* (London: Random House, 2017); Redman, "How Accurate Are Eyewitnesses?,"; McIver, "Eyewitnesses as Guarantors," esp. pp. 530–533.

96 McIver, "Eyewitnesses as Guarantors," pp. 534–535.

97 Rodney Stark, *The Triumph of Christianity: How the Jesus Movement Became the World's Largest Religion* (New York: HarperOne, 2011), pp. 155–157.

98 Stark, *Triumph*, p. 156.

99 Robert McIver, *Memory, Jesus, and the Synoptic Gospels* (Atlanta, GA: SBL, 2011), p. 206. These statistics focus mainly on Capernaum and Jerusalem, however, and include casual bystanders to Jesus' public ministry.

100 See Richard Bauckham, *The Gospels for All Christians: Rethinking the Gospel Audiences*, ed. Richard Bauckham (Grand Rapids, Mich: W.B. Eerdmans, 1998), pp. 30–34; See also, Michael B. Thompson, "The Holy Internet: Communication between Churches in the First Christian Generation," in *The Gospels for All Christians*, pp. 49–70.

101 Richard Glover, "Luke the Antiochene and Acts," *NTS* 11.1 (1964), pp. 97–106, esp. p. 103. This point cannot be pressed too far since incidental names are also mentioned in lodgings not in the "we" sections (cf. Acts 12.12; 18.7). This does not exclude the possibility that some of these other names were also sources, however, though not part of a "we" narrative. Colin Hemer considers various incidental names outside of the "we" sections as possible allusions to informants (John and Alexander, Acts 4.6; Rhoda, 12.13–17; Blastus, 12.20; etc.). See Colin Hemer, *The Book of Acts in the Setting of Hellenistic History*, WUNT 49 (Tübingen: Mohr Siebeck, 1989), p. 208.

102 See Hemer, *Acts*, pp. 335–363.

103 Albert Hogeterp and Adelbert Denaux, *Semitisms in Luke's Greek: A Descriptive Analysis of Lexical and Syntactical Domains of Semitic Language Influence in Luke's Gospel*, WUNT 401 (Tübingen: Mohr Siebeck, 2018).

104 Craig Blomberg, *BBR* 291 (2019), pp. 105–106.

105 Hogeterp and Denaux conclude their study: "With details of Semitic language and tradition backgrounds, Luke buttresses the point of authenticity and reliability of his gospel account about Jesus and his movement in the early Jewish milieus of first century C. E. Israel. It may be added that literary code-switching in Luke-Acts, as hypothesized by J.M Watt, also underlines the correlation between a Jewish setting and a Semitized Greek variety of language as a literary procedure" (*Semitisms in Luke's Greek*, p. 505).

106 See David Moessner, *Luke the Historian of Israel's Legacy, Theologian of Israel's 'Christ'* (Berlin, Boston: De Gruyter, 2016), pp. 108–123; Robert Tannehill, *The Narrative Unity of Luke-Acts: A Literary Interpretation* (Vol. 1; Philadelphia, PA: Fortress Press, 1991), pp. 9–12; M. Völkel, "Exegetische Erwägungen zum Verständis des Begriffs καθεξῆς im lukanischen Prolog," *NTS* 20 (1973/4), pp. 289–299, esp. 293.

107 For (καί) ἐγένετο (δὲ) as a structural marker, see J. A. Gault, "The Discourse Function of kai egeneto in Luke and Acts," *OPTAT* 4 (1990), pp. 388–399. ἐγένετο constructions occur in narrative text 37 times out of a total of 39 usages, according to Hogeterp and Denaux, often followed by ἐν τῷ + infinitive. Καί ἰδοῦ occurs in narrative frameworks 15 of 26 times (*Semitisms*, pp. 496–497). Michael Wolter remarks, "The most conspicuous features of the Lukan style of narration include—even more than in Acts—the imitation of the language of the Old Testament, namely in its Greek translation, the Septuagint," and he goes on to mention the previous Semitisms and others also mentioned by Denaux and Hogeterp (*The Gospel According to Luke—Volume I (1–9.50)*. Eds. Wayne Coppins, Simon Gathercole; trans. by Wayne Coppins, Christoph Heilig. BMSEC 4. (Waco, Tex.: Baylor University Press, 2016), p. 25). For a contrary view, see Randall Buth, "Distinguishing Hebrew from Aramaic in Semitized Greek Texts, with an Application for the Gospels and

Pseudepigrapha" in *The Language Environment of First Century Judaea* (Leiden, The Netherlands: Brill, 2014), pp. 310–314.

108 Any errors in Appendix B are likely the result of my transcription; upon my review, I removed a few Semitisms that may have been incorrectly referenced by Denaux and Hogeterp.

109 Due to the volume of Semitisms therein, the Infancy Narrative (Luke 1–2) is excluded from this figure.

110 This is especially if one translates πεπληροφορημένων in terms of "fulfillment" versus mere "accomplishment." Against the common translation of πεπληροφορημένων in terms of "fulfillment" (followed by NIV, NKJV, NRS, CSB, but not by ESV, NASB, RSV), see Kenneth Litwak, "ΠΕΡΙ ΤΩΝ ΠΕΠΛΗΡΟΦΟΡΗΜΕΝΩΝ ΕΝ ΗΜΙΝ ΠΡΓΜΑΤΩΝ: Concerning the Things Fulfilled or Accomplished?," *RevBib* 113.1 (2006), pp. 37–52.

111 Yet many intertextual parallels do not align programmatically with any overriding theological theme. Thomas Brodie highlights parallels between portions of Luke and the Elijah/Elisha narratives, but he has failed to convince scholars that this demonstrates any programmatic function for Luke's main structure (see the full discussion in John Kloppenborg & Joseph Verheyden, (Eds.). *The Elijah-Elisha Narrative in the Composition of Luke* (The Library of New Testament Studies, London: Bloomsbury Academic, 2005). Craig Evans, likewise, highlights parallels ("Luke's Use of the Elijah/Elisha Narratives and the Ethic of Election," *JBL* 106.1 (1987), pp. 75–83; Craig Evans, James A. Sanders, *Luke and Scripture: The Function of Sacred Tradition in Luke-Acts* (Eugene, OR: Wipf and Stock Publishers, 2001), as does David Moessner (e.g., "'The Christ Must Suffer': New Light On the Jesus-Peter, Stephen, Paul Parallels in Luke-Acts," *NovTest* 28 (1986), pp. 220–256), but none of these parallels align either individually or collectively with Luke's structured Semitisms. This is not to deny that parallels exist but merely to point out that they do not seem to function as the main influence behind how Luke patterned his Septuagintal language throughout Luke-Acts.

112 I.e., λέγεται, *Thuc.* 2.93.4, 3.79.3; κατά τοῦτον τόν καιρὸν, Josephus, *Ant.* 9.239–242, 11.304, 12.354–359, etc. On Josephus' source citations, see the discussion by Daniel Schwartz, "Kata Toyton Ton Kai-

pon: Josephus' Source on Agrippa II," *The Jewish Quarterly Review* 72.4 (1982), pp. 241–268.

113 A specific example might be how Luke revises the transfiguration account to highlight the experience as a divine visitation, in line with his broader agenda to craft Jesus' journey to Jerusalem in terms of Yahweh's visitation of his temple; see Gregory R. Lanier, "Luke's Distinctive Use of the Temple: Portraying the Divine Visitation," *JTS* 65.2 (2014), pp. 433–462.

114 See Richard Bauckham's discussion in *Jesus and the Eyewitnesses*, pp. 525–527.

115 See Donald Earl, "Prologue-Form in Ancient Historiography," *ANRW* 1 (1972), pp. 842–856, esp. 855 and Zachary Dawson, "Does Luke's Preface Resemble a Greek Decree? Comparing the Epigraphical and Papyrological Evidence of Greek Decrees with Ancient Preface Formulae," *NTS* 65 (2019), pp. 552–571, esp. 557.

116 I agree with John Robinson's position, although this remains a minority perspective: "The author of Acts is an independent lay mind of Gentile upbringing who presents himself (Luke 1.1–4) *primarily* as an historian, not a professional theologian…The recent tendency to turn Luke into a 'theologian's theologian', is, I believe, a misguided exercise and detracts from the appreciation of his stated purpose and, within his own terms, still profoundly theological understanding of events [emphasis in the original]" (*Redating the New Testament* (Eugene, OR: Wipf and Stock Publishers, 1976), p. 87).

117 See the comments by Delbert Burkett, "Jesus in Luke-Acts," in *The Blackwell Companion to Jesus*, ed. D. Burkett (London: Wiley-Blackwell, 2011), esp. p. 47.

118 Luke's syntax appears to treat them as one group in Luke 1.2.

119 In Luke's Gospel the ὑπηρέτης (Luke 4.20), the presence of whom has also been confirmed by Roman epigraphy (*CIJ* I² 172 = Noy, *JIWE* 2 290), was the individual who handled the word of God (i.e., the Torah scrolls), equivalent to the Hebrew *hazzan* or the pagan temple attendant (νεωκόπος). Throughout Luke-Acts, Luke consistently equates the Gospel message with the word of God.

120 James A. Sanders, "Isaiah in Luke," *Interpretation* 36.2 (1982), pp. 144–155, esp. 149.

121 Willy Lindwer, *The Last Seven Months of Anne Frank* (New York: 1st Anchor Books, 1992), xi.

122 Author's translation.

123 Due to the volume of references, I will not be able to make specific citations to Lindwer's *The Last Seven Months* when comparing the interviews, although his work can be easily consulted. This lack of precision in citation is not unusual. The study from Wagenaar and Groeneweg ("The Memory of Concentration Camp Survivors"), for example, cited by both Volbert ("Aussagen über traumatische Erlebnisse") and McIver (*Memory*, pp. 55–56) lacks many details one might be interested in without references to allow for further inquiry. Since I initially considered using Wageneer and Groeneweg's primary sources for this research project I tried to retrieve these by contacting Professor Groeneweg, but he was no longer able to access the data from the interviews referenced in his study. The benefit of our exercise is that Lindwer's published work provides a readily accessible primary source for anyone interested. The supplemental oral history interviews can be found in *The Jeff and Toby Herr Oral History Archive*: "Interview with Helen Waterford" (March 12, 1992) Accession Number: 1994. A.0447.29, RG Number: RG-50.042.0029; "Interview with Eva Schloss" (May 11, 1999) Accession Number: 1999. A.0261, RG Number: RG-50.485.0001. These are made available by the United States Holocaust Memorial Museum and can be accessed online at https://collections.ushmm.org/search/?f[special_collection][]=The+Jeff+and+Toby+Herr+Oral+History+Archive.

124 Lindwer, *Last Seven Months*, p. ix.

125 See Richard Bauckham's helpful discussion on the relationship between the Gospels and the testimonies of Holocaust survivors in *Jesus and the Eyewitnesses*, pp. 501–502.

126 Keener, *Christobiography*, p. 441.

127 Ibid., Ch. 15, "Jesus was a Teacher," pp. 401–448; cf., Paul Rhodes Eddy and Gregory Boyd. *The Jesus Legend: A Case for the Historical Reliability of the Synoptic Jesus Tradition* (Grand Rapids: Baker Academic, 2007), pp. 269–306.

128 Lindmer, *Final Seven Months*, p. 8.

129 These radically different interpretations between JB and LJ may shed light on divergent points of emphasis between Acts and Paul's letters.

130 See Gathercole, "Alleged Anonymity," p. 462 n. 56; F. Gerald Downing, "Redaction Criticism: Josephus' Antiquities and the Synoptic Gospels (II)," *JSNT* 9.3 (1980), pp. 29–48, esp. 33; Joseph Fitzmyer, *The Gospel According to Luke I-IX: A New Translation with Introduction and Commentary* (Garden City, NY: Doubleday & Co.: 1985), pp. 107–108.

131 Luke Timothy Johnson, *Prophetic Jesus, Prophetic Church: The Challenge of Luke-Acts to Contemporary Christians* (Kindle Locations 197–199), Kindle edition.

132 Fitzmyer, *The Gospel According to Luke*, pp. 92–96.

133 See Slawomir Szkredka, "The Call of Simon Peter in Luke 5.1–11: A Lukan Invention?," *BibAn* 8.2 (2018), pp. 173–189; R. Steven Notley, "The Sea of Galilee. Development of an Early Christian Toponym," *JBL* 128.1 (2009), pp. 183–188, esp. 184; Gerd Theissen, "Meer und See in den Evangelien. Ein Beitrag zur. Lokalkoloritforschung," SNTU 10 (1985), pp. 5–25, esp. 11–12.

134 Theissen suggests Luke picked up the toponym in Jerusalem prior to 70 CE, "Meer und See," p. 11; Szkredka, "The Call," suggests it derived from a source that combined the catch of fish with the call of Peter.

135 See David Alan Black, "New Testament Semitisms," *The Bible Translator* 39.2 (April 1988), pp. 215–223, esp. 221.

136 For Hemer's similar analysis of this passage and his reflections on Peter's possible role as informant, see: *The Book of Acts*, pp. 356–358.

137 *Thuc.* 1.1.5; 4.2.2. The reference is only a point of comparison; I do not mean to imply imitation.

138 Mark's account in Jericho from its inception is told from the perspective of blind Bartimaeus (Mark 10.46–51); for an excellent discussion, see Richard Bauckham, "Eyewitnesses and Healing Miracles in the Gospel of Mark," *BibAn* 10.3 (2020), pp. 341–354, esp. 351.

139 Bauckham, *Jesus and the Eyewitnesses*, p. 55.

140 Williams, *Can We Trust the Gospels?*, pp. 82–84; Babylonian Talmud *Pesachim* 57a.

141 See Licona, *Why Are There Differences in the Gospels?*, p. 173.

142 Pär-Anders Granhag et al., "Partners in Crime: How Liars in Collusion Betray Themselves," *Journal of Applied Psychology* 33.4 (2003), pp. 848–868, esp. 863.

143 See Craig Keener and Edward Wright, eds., *Biographies and Jesus: What Does it Mean for the Gospels to be Biographies?* (Lexington, KY: Emeth Press, 2016), p. 162.

144 See Lydia McGrew on this point: *The Mirror or the Mask*, pp. 236–239.

145 Christopher Pelling, "Plutarch's Adaptation of his Source Material," *JHS* 20 (1980), pp. 127–140; Brad Cook, "Plutarch's Use of Legetai: Narrative Design and Source in Alexander," *Greek, Roman and Byzantine Studies* 42.4 (Winter 2001), pp. 329–360.

146 As Notley ("The Sea," pp. 185–186) has argued, the Markan/Matthean/Johannine toponym θάλασσα τῆς Γαλιλαίας (Matt 4.18; 15.29; Mark 1.16; 7.31; John 6.1) —elsewhere unattested—likely results from theological motivations, i.e., to highlight Jesus' fulfillment of Isa 8.23 [Eng. 9.1] (cf. Matt 4:12b–16, 18): "…He withdrew *into Galilee*; and leaving Nazareth he went and dwelt in Capernaum by the sea, *in the territory of Zebulun and Naphtali*, that what was spoken by the prophet Isaiah might be fulfilled: *Land of Zebulun and land of Naphtali, the way to the sea*, along the Jordan, *Galilee of the Gentiles*, the people living in darkness have seen a great light; on those living in the land of the shadow of death a light has dawned…As he walked by *the Sea of Galilee*."

147 See McGrew, *In Plain View*, pp. 17–25. Regarding an attack on the Roman Senate during the reign of Otho, for example, the account of Suetonius (*Otho* 8.2) makes the description of the same event from Tacitus intelligible (*Hist.* 1.80); see Keener and Wright, *Biographies and Jesus*, p. 156.

148 Part of this chapter is reproduced in my article, "The Beloved Eyewitness," *NTS* 68.3 (2022), pp. 351–57.

149 See, for example, John 2.21, 8.58, and 20.31.

150 For a good discussion of this movement, see Paul Anderson, "Jesus in Johannine Perspective: Inviting a Fourth Quest for Jesus," *Conspectus* 32.1 (October 2021), pp. 7–41.

151 This illustration was first published in *Puck*, an American humor magazine, on 6 November 1915, and is part of the Public Domain.

152 Michael Nicholls et al., "Perception of an Ambiguous Figure is Affected by Own-age Social Bias," *Scientific Reports* 8.1 (2018), 12661.

153 E. Bialystok and D. Shapero, "Ambiguous Benefits: The Effect of Bilingualism on Reversing Ambiguous Figures," *Developmental Science* 8 (2005), pp. 595–604.

154 Pierson Parker, "Luke and the Fourth Evangelist," *NTS* 9.4 (1963), pp. 317–336, esp. 335.

155 Van de Weghe, "The Beloved Eyewitness."

156 Parker, "The Fourth Evangelist," p. 331. Emphasis also in the original.

157 F. Lamar Cribbs, "St. Luke and the Johannine Tradition," *JBL* 90.4 (1971), pp. 422–450, esp. 447.

158 Granted, the Beloved Disciple's presence can also be inferred in other portions (e.g., the Upper Room discourse), but the point remains that many portions of the Fourth Gospel omit the implication—and these are the very portions the Third Evangelist shares little material with.

159 See Derek Tovey, *Narrative Art and Act in the Fourth Gospel* (Sheffield: Sheffield Academic, 1997), p. 140.

160 Pierson Parker, "Two Editions of John," *JBL* 75 (1956), pp. 303–314; Cribbs, "Johannine Tradition," pp. 449–450; Mark Matson, *In Dialogue with Another Gospel? The Influence of the Fourth Gospel on the Passion Narrative of the Gospel of Luke in SBL Dissertation Series 187* (Atlanta: SBL, 1998), pp. 446–448; Marie-Émile Boismard and A. Lamouille, *L'Evangile de Jean: Synopse de quatre evangiles en français* (Paris: Éd. du Cerf, 1977); see also, D. Moody Smith's comments in "John and the Synoptics," *Bib* 63 (1982), pp. 102–113; see also, Anderson's comments in "Inviting a Fourth Quest," pp. 20–23.

161 Prior to the printing press, early drafts/editions to compositions were not generally circulated. Keener writes: "In our view, if the Gospel had an earlier form (aside from its early draft stage, which was probably not circulated), it may have been the oral form in which the beloved disciple and/or the Fourth Evangelist preached it" (Craig Keener, *The Gospel of John: A Commentary* (Peabody, PA: Hendrickson, 2003), p. 38. Clement of Alexandria's comment (Eusebius, *Hist. Eccl.* 3.24.1–13) also supports a prior oral stage. It is further possible the Fourth Evangelist based his narrative on earlier memoirs from the Beloved Disciple but was distinct from him (cf. R. Alan Culpepper, *Anatomy of the Fourth Gospel: A Study in Literary Design* (Philadelphia: Fortress, 1983)), yet Bauckham's arguments for the work's unity and the author's direct claim to eyewitness testimony are compelling ("The 153 Fish and the Unity of the Fourth Gospel," *NeoTest* 36.1 (2002), pp. 77–88).

162 This is congruent with the "mediating view" of John's interlocking relationship with the Synoptics in which the author's knowledge of them is assumed on some level (and/or knowledge of pre-synoptic traditions), but is not directly dependent upon the Synoptics literarily, sometimes conflicting with but also incidentally corroborating/explaining Synoptic details. See James Dvorak, "The Relationship Between John and the Synoptics," *JETS* 41.2 (1998), pp. 201–213, esp. 211–213.

163 For this preference among ancient historians, see: Peters, "Source Claims"; Byrskog, *Story*, pp. 49–91; Schepens, "History and *Historia*: Inquiry in the Greek Historians"; Marincola, *Authority and Tradition in Ancient Historiography*; our discussion in Chapter 1.

164 The significance of these initial observations depends, of course, on two controversial assumptions in New Testament scholarship: that the author of the Fourth Gospel is the Beloved Disciple, and that the Beloved Disciple is John son of Zebedee.

165 Rainer Riesner, "John 1.14 and 'the Disciple whom Jesus loved'," in *Rediscovering John: Essays on the Fourth Gospel in Honour of Frédéric Manns*, Ed. L. Daniel Chrupcala. (SBFA 80; Jerusalem: Edizioni Terra Santa, 2013), pp. 303–336, esp. 311–312.

166 Most commentators delineate the Travel Narrative as Luke 9.51–19.44 (see the discussion in Adelbert Denaux, "The Delineation of the

Lukan Travel Narrative within the overall Structure of the Gospel of Luke," in Camille Focant (ed.), *The Synoptic Gospels. Source Criticism and the New Literary Criticism*, BETL 110 (Leuven: Leuven University Press, 1993), pp. 359–392). Our focus on issues within Luke 9.51–18.15 is determined by source-critical considerations (i.e., this is the uniquely non-Markan section) and by the fact that Luke's geographical oddities are bound to this section of the narrative. The delineation of the Great Interpolation as being equivalent to the Travel Narrative was held by many older commentators (e.g., Wilhelm M. L. de Wette, *Erklärung des Lukas und Markus* (Leipzig: Weidmannsche Buchhandlung, 1836); Burnette H. Streeter, *The Four Gospels: A Study of Origins* (London: MacMillan & Co. Ltd., 1924), p. 203).

167 David Gill, "Observations on the Lukan Travel Narrative and Some Related Passages," *HTR* 63.2 (1970), pp. 199–221, esp. 199.

168 Bock, *Luke,* p. 960.

169 Even William Arndt, who attempts to harmonize Luke's narrative with the chronology of the Fourth Gospel, argues for several journeys (William F. Arndt, *The Gospel according to St. Luke* (St. Louis: Concordia, 1956), p. 272), as does Louis Girard, *L'Evangile des voyages de Jésus ou la section 9,51–18,14 de Saint Luc* (Paris: Gabalda, 1951). G. Ogg argues for a single chronological journey, although he believes this same journey is recounted twice, at the bookends of the Travel Narrative ("The Central Section of the Gospel according to Luke," *NTS* 18 (1971), pp. 39–53).

170 J. A. Robertson, "The Passion Journey," *Expositor* 8.17 (1919), 54–55. See also: C. C. McCown, "The Geography of Luke's Central Section," *JBL* 6 (1938), pp. 51–66.

171 In the Fourth Gospel, the raising of Lazarus instigates the plot to kill Jesus (John 11.45–57), happening sometime during the last several months of Jesus' life (cf. the timeline implied by John 10.22, 11.54, etc.) and is seemingly orchestrated by Jesus despite its foreseen consequences (cf., John 10.11; 11.6; 12.7–9; 12.23–26; see also, references to the ὥρα of Jesus, John 7.6, 7.30, 8.20, 12.23). The Lukan Travel Narrative is structured around an inevitable journey to Jerusalem that leads to Jesus' ἔξοδος (Luke 9.31).

172 The point is not to deny the presence of a "prophet-like-Moses" motif in Luke-Acts and in the traditions of Jesus in general. See Scot McKnight, "Jesus and Prophetic Actions," *BBR* 10.2 (2000), pp. 197–232.

173 Thomas Brodie, "The Departure for Jerusalem (Luke 9,51–56) as a Rhetorical Imitation of Elijah's Departure for the Jordan (2 Kgs 1,1–2,6)," *Bib* 70.1 (1989), pp. 96–109, esp. 103.

174 See, however, Jeremy Otten's careful discussion on the Jesus-Elijah relationship in Luke: "The Bad Samaritans: The Elijah Motif in Luke 9.51–56," *JSNT* 42.3 (2020), pp. 375–389.

175 Brodie, "The Departure," p. 100.

176 Some conjecture is unavoidable, as with the directionality of Jesus' travels along the border of Samaria and Galilee before he inevitably ends up in Jericho, where Luke reconnects geographically with his Markan template (Luke 18.35; cf. Mark 10.46). Likewise, this route was retained for Elisha's journey due to his tendency to lodge in Shunem during his travels (2 Kings 2:8). Shunem was located at the eastern portion of what later would become the border of Samaria and Galilee.

177 E.g., by the time of the NT, Bethel had faded into obscurity relative to Jerusalem. I place the Gilgal of 2 Kings 2.1 on the map at the approximate location of *Jiljilya* about 7.5 miles N of Bethel in the Central Hills. This general location has been suggested by various previous and contemporary scholars based on the comment that Elijah/Elijah went "down" to Bethel, indicating a location for Gilgal nearby Bethel but at a higher elevation. The possibility of this solution is hinted at as early as Eusebius and Jerome (Euseb. *Onom.* 66.6–7). The earliest modern treatment of *Jiljilya* as Gilgal is Eli Smith, "List of Arabic Names of Places in Palestine and the Adjacent Regions," in Edward Robinson and Eli Smith (eds.) *Biblical Researches in Palestine, Mount Sinai and Arabia Petraea. A Journal of Travels in the Year 1838* (London: Crocker & Brewster, 1841), pp. 112–196, esp. 145; see also, Siegfried Mittmann and Gotz Schmitt, eds., *Tübinger Bibelatlas* (Stuttgart: Deutsche Bibelgesellschaft, 2001), BX 12: 1712.1598; O. Thenius, *Die Bücher der Könige* (2nd ed.; Leipzig: S. Hirzel, 1873), pp. 270–271; W. R. Kotter, "Gilgal," *ABD* 2 (1992), p. 1023; Jesse C. Long, *1 & 2 Kings* (College Press NIV Commentary; Joplin, MO: College Press, 2002), p. 287. Likewise, John

11.54's Ephraim cannot be located with certainty, but I place it approximately at modern-day et-Taiyiba.

178 THGNT.

179 Author's translation.

180 Conditions in rural Galilee were likely dire. Sakari Häkkinen writes, "First-century Galilee was mainly agricultural, with little fishing industry, and its population was economically strongly dependent on the wealthy elite, the majority of whom lived in Sepphoris and Tiberias, some even in Jerusalem. The elite lived by depriving the Galilean rural population, with no direct connection to the ordinary people. Their agents collected taxes, and usually the villagers had the opportunity to deal with minor legal things themselves in local assemblies, the synagogues. The poverty in Galilee is also reflected by the fact that almost no remains of storage buildings for grain or other products have been found in archaeological excavations in Galilee and no shops at all. The Galileans seem to have consumed all they produced. Having paid the rents, taxes, loan remissions and interests there simply was nothing left to trade with" (Sakari Häkkinen, "Poverty in the first-century Galilee," *HTS* 72.4 (2016), pp. 1–9, esp. 7).

181 My observations here are indebted to many helpful studies: see, for example: Caleb C. Afulike "Luke's Portrayal of the Social Dimension in the Ministry of Jesus and the Apostles (Luke-Acts) According to Isaiah's Message of Social Justice in Chapters 61.1–2 and 58.6," *Journal of Religious & Theological Information* 17.2 (2018), pp. 41–54; Paul Hertig, "The Jubilee Mission of Jesus in the Gospel of Luke: Reversals of Fortunes," *Missiology* 26.2 (1998), pp. 167–179; David Hill, "The Rejection of Jesus at Nazareth (Luke 4.16–30)," *NovT* 13.3 (1971), pp. 161–180; Sanders, "Isaiah in Luke," pp. 154–155.

182 Graham Twelftree, *Jesus the Miracle Worker: A Historical and Theological Study* (Downers Grove, IL: Intervarsity Press, 1999), pp. 173–174.

183 D. Gerald Bostock, "Jesus as the New Elisha," *ExpT* 92.2 (November 1980), pp. 39–41.

184 See Paul Barnett, "The Jewish Sign Prophets—A.D. 40–70: Their Intentions and Origin," *NTS* 27.5 (1981), pp. 679–697.

185 Portions of this chapter and the next are reproduced in my broader discussion on the historical and theological interplay of Luke's Christology, "Early Divine Christology: Scripture, Narrativity and Confession in Luke-Acts" in *Scripture and Theology: Historical and Systematic Perspectives* (eds., T. Bokedal, L. Jansen, and M. Borowski; to be published by De Gruyter).

186 For the centrality of the cross in John's Gospel, see my article, co-authored with John Battle, "Truth and Semantic Change in the Gospel of John," *BBR* 31.2 (2021), pp. 211–227.

187 This illustration is taken from McGrew, *Undesigned Coincidences*, pp. 49–51, 68–70.

188 For a brief discussion on this by Richard Bauckham, see "The Relatives of Jesus," *Themelios* 21.2 (January 1996), pp. 18–21; for a longer discussion, see Bauckham, *Jude and the Relatives of Jesus in the Early Church* (Edinburgh: T&T Clark, 1990), Ch. 7.

189 C. Blumenthal, "Augustus' Erlass und Gottes Macht: Überlegungen zur Charakterisierung der Augustusfigur und ihrer erzählstrategischen Funktion in der lukanischen Erzählung," *NTS* 57.1 (2011), pp. 1–30; Michael Kochenash, "'Adam, Son of God' (Luke 3.38): Another Jesus–Augustus Parallel in Luke's Gospel," *NTS* 64.3 (2018), pp. 307–325; Bradly Billings, "'At the Age of 12': The Boy Jesus in the Temple (Luke 2.41–52), The Emperor Augustus, and the Social Setting of the Third Gospel," *JTS* 60.1 (April 2009), pp. 70–89.

190 For further discussion, see: Joel Green, "The Social Status of Mary in Luke 1,5–2,52: A Plea for Methodological Integration," *Bib* 73.4 (1992), pp. 457–472.

191 Edward Meadors, "Isaiah 40.3 and the Synoptic Gospels' Parody of the Roman Road System," *NTS* 66.1 (2020), pp. 106–124.

192 Royce Morris, "Why ΑΥΓΟΥΣΤΟΣ? A Note to Luke 2.1," *NTS* 38.1 (1992), pp. 142–144.

193 See Friedrich Blass and Albert Debrunner, *A Greek Grammar of the New Testament and Other Early Christian Literature*, translated by Robert W. Funk (Chicago: Chicago University Press, 1964), p. 4; cited by Morris, "A Note to Luke 2.1," p. 143.

194 The transliteration does not occur in Greek writings prior to Luke and nowhere in the papyri prior to 223 CE; indeed, Morris notes: "that it later became a proper name is not in dispute; but it is clearly apparent that it became a proper name because of Luke's use of the word in the Gospel, and it also seems obvious that it became a proper name because it was unintelligible otherwise to his Greek audience" ("A Note to Luke 2.1," p. 143).

195 For a historical study of Mary and Joseph's lodgings, see Stephen Carlson, "The Accommodations of Joseph and Mary in Bethlehem: Κατάλυμα in Luke 2.7," *NTS* 56.3 (2010), pp. 326–342. Much has been written on the relationship between Luke and Rome: e.g., C. Kavin Rowe, "Luke-Acts and the Imperial Cult: A Way Through the Conundrum?," *JSNT* 27.3 (2005), pp. 279–300; Paul W. Walaskay, "The Trial and Death of Jesus in the Gospel of Luke," *JBL* 94.1 (1975), pp. 81–93; Michael Kochenash, "Taking the Bad with the Good: Reconciling Images of Rome in Luke–Acts," *RSR* 41.2 (2015), pp. 43–51.

196 Simon Gathercole, "The Heavenly ἀνατολή (Luke 1.78–9)," *JTS* 65.2 (October 2005), pp. 471–488.

197 For further discussion on this, see: Brendan Byrne, "Jesus as Messiah in the Gospel of Luke: Discerning a Pattern of Correction," *CBQ* 65.1 (2003), pp. 80–95, esp. 84–86. This study demonstrates how Luke shows Jesus to be a transcendent Messiah by subtle redactions/features which correct possible perceptions that Jesus' charges—that he was a messianic pretender—might have been justified.

198 Richard Hays comments, "Luke's extended citation of Isaiah 40.3–5 functions as a programmatic introduction to the narrative of Jesus' ministry (Luke 3.4–6); it frames his activity in terms of Isaiah's visionary prophecy of the end of Israel's exile and thereby serves as a 'hermeneutical key for the Lukan program.' Particularly significant is the fact that Luke concludes his citation of Isaiah 40 with the climactic declaration that 'all flesh will see the salvation of God.' ... Luke has taken the keynote passage from Isaiah 40 that declares the salvific coming of Israel's God and worked it narratively into an announcement of the imminent coming of Jesus as the one who would bring 'the salvation of God' (3.6, citing Isa 40: 5 LXX). Luke's citation of the extended block of material from Isaiah 40: 3–5 strongly suggests

that he is aware of the full context of Isaiah 40. If so, this identification of Jesus as the one in whom 'all flesh will see the salvation of God' is hermeneutically momentous, for it is precisely in Isaiah 40 that we find one of the most radical declarations in all of Scripture of the incomparability of God…" (Richard B. Hays, *Reading Backwards* (Waco, TX: Baylor University Press, 2014), pp. 63–64).

199 Isaiah 6.1–8 and Luke 5.1–11 are, indeed, paired together in the Revised Common Lectionary. For further discussions on the connection, see Richard B. Hays, "Netted," in *The Art of Reading Scripture* (eds. Ellen F. Davis and Richard B. Hays; Grand Rapids: Eerdmans, 2003), pp. 311–316; C. Kavin Rowe, *Early Narrative Christology: The Lord in the Gospel of Luke* (BZNW 139; Berlin and New York: de Gruyter, 2006), p. 99.

200 The event was significant to the early church and appears to have played a legitimizing role for the Sons of Zebedee and Simon Peter; see David Wenham and A. D. A. Moses, "'There Are Some Standing Here…': Did They Become the 'Reputed Pillars' of the Jerusalem Church? Some Reflections on Mark 9.1, Galatians 2.9 and the Transfiguration," *NovT* 36.2 (1994), pp. 146–163.

201 Heinz Schürmann, *Das Lukasevangelium: Kommentar zu Kap. 1,1–9,50*, Vol. 1 (HTKNT 3/1; 4th ed.; Freiburg: Herder, 1990), pp. 556–557; John P. Heil, *The Transfiguration of Jesus Narrative Meaning and Function of Mark 9.2–8, Matt 1 7.1–8 and Luke 9.28–36* (AnBib 144; Rome Pontificio Istituto Biblico, 2000), p. 272; David Miller, "Seeing the Glory, Hearing the Son: The Function of the Wilderness Theophany Narratives in Luke 9: 28–36," *CBQ* 72.3 (2010), pp. 498–517; Lanier, "Luke's Distinctive Use of the Temple."

202 Miller, "Hearing the Son," p. 503; Lanier, "Portraying the Divine Visitation," pp. 451–452.

203 Miller, "Hearing the Son," p. 502.

204 François Bovon, *L'Évangile selon Saint Luc 1–9* (Gèneve: Labor et Fides, 1991), pp. 488–489; Robert O'Toole states that this is a reference to the Hebrew text of Isaiah 42.1 (Robert O'Toole, "How Does Luke Portray Jesus as Servant of Yhwh," *Bib* 81.3 (2000), pp. 328–346); That Luke quotes texts aligned more closely with the Proto-MT has recently

been suggested by Kai Akagi, "Luke 1.49 and the Form of Isaiah in Luke: An Overlooked Allusion and the Problem of an Assumed LXX Text," *JBL* 138.1 (2019), pp. 183–201, see esp. 192–193.

205 This comes at the end of a masterful literary parallel drawn between Barabbas and the crowd to emphasize Jesus' substitutionary death (see the excellent article by Monique Cuany, "Jesus, Barabbas and the People: The Climax of Luke's Trial Narrative and Lukan Christology (Luke 23.13–25)," *JSNT* 39.4 (2017), pp. 441–458. Given that Luke uses narrative technique here to highlight Jesus' substitutionary atonement, as well as allusions to Isaiah 53 and other Isaianic servant passages, it is all the more puzzling why Luke would neglect to include Mark 10.45 if he wished to emphasize this theme. For a reasonable solution, see: David Moffitt, "Atonement at the Right Hand: The Sacrificial Significance of Jesus' Exaltation in Acts," *NTS* 62.4 (2016), pp. 549–568.

206 τῇ συνέσει δικαιῶσαι δίκαιον εὖ δουλεύοντα πολλοῖς, LXX; cf. Luke 23:47b, Acts 3.14, 26.

207 For another argument favoring yet another connection to the Elisha narrative (2 Kings 5.8–19) with this pericope, see: Wilhelm Bruners, *Die Reinigung der zehn Aussätzigen und die Heilung des Samariters, Lk 17,11–19: Ein Beitrag zur lukanischen Interpretation der Reinigung von Aussätzigen* (FB 23; Stuttgart: Katholisches Bibelwerk, 1977). Our brief discussion leans on Dennis Hamm's article, "What the Samaritan Leper Sees: The Narrative Christology of Luke 17.11–19," *CBQ* 56.2 (1994), pp. 273–287.

208 After surveying the relevant literature on the Samaritans, Hamm comments: "Quite strikingly, what one learns from a reading of our information about Samaritans amounts to the very same three themes evoked in John 4: (1) Samaritans and Jews share a common tradition (the Torah and a claim to descend from Abraham); (2) they have a history of enmity; and (3) they are divided mainly by the concern for the right place to worship Yahweh—Jerusalem or Gerizim. This preoccupation with the right place to worship the Hebrew God may be the main thing we need to know to understand Luke's special interest in the ethnicity of the grateful leper" ("What the Samaritan Leper Sees," p. 282).

209 Ibid., p. 284.

210 Trevor J. Burke, "The Parable of the Prodigal Father: An Interpretative Key to the Third Gospel (Luke 15.11–32)," *TynBul* 64.2 (2013), pp. 17–38.

211 Kenneth Bailey, *The Cross and the Prodigal: The 15th Chapter of Luke, Seen through the Eyes of Middle Eastern Peasants* (St. Louis, MO: Concordia Publishing House, 1973; 2nd edition, Downers Grove, IL: InterVarsity Press, 2005).

212 Kenneth Bailey, *Finding the Lost Cultural Keys to Luke 15* (Concordia Scholarship Today: Concordia Publishing House, 2005), pp. 132–150.

213 Maarten Menken, "The Position of σπλαγχνίζεσθαι and σπλάγχνα in the Gospel of Luke," *NovTest* (1988), pp. 107–114, esp. 113.

214 Bailey, *Finding the Lost*, p. 189.

215 Ibid., p. 151.

216 Credit for this illustration goes to Dr. John Battle from Western Reformed Seminary.

217 For a discussion of this and the revolutionary message of Christianity, see Tom Holland, *Dominion: How the Christian Revolution Remade the World* (NY: Basic Books, 2019), esp. pp. 6, 80–106.

218 Tables of named persons, anonymous persons, toponyms, and their in-text references are available for any of the works discussed upon request. See my *NTS* article, "The Beloved Eyewitness," for my contact information.

219 Strickland, "What's in a Name?," p. 36; cf. Bauckham, *Jesus and the Eyewitnesses*, p. 88 (1st ed.); Bauckham did not correct this for his second edition, in which the error occurs again in Table 6 on p. 84.

220 I.e., I would classify the name which qualifies the Simon of the Gospels (Peter/Petra—"the rock") as a standardized nickname while discounting the qualifier attached to Barsabas Justus in the Acts of Paul ("of the Broad Feet").

221 See, for example, the remarks in endnote 53 of Chapter 2.

222 Bauckham, *Jesus and the Eyewitnesses*, pp. 67–68; Ilan I, p. 1.

223 Peter Fraser and Elaine Matthews (ed.), *A Lexicon of Greek Personal Names* (5 Vols.; Oxford: Clarendon, 1987–2014).

224 *Prosopographia Imperii Romani Saec I, II, III.* Partim consilio et auctoritate Academiae Scientiarum Regiae Borussicae editum. Partim consilio et auctoritate Academiae Scientiarum Rei Publicae Democraticae Germanicae editum. Editio altera (Berlin, Boston: De Gruyter, n.d.).

225 T. Robert S. Broughton's *The Magistrates of the Roman Republic* (New York: American Philological Association, 1951) provides the backbone for the database. That the PIR and DPRR focus only on elite persons would skew our analysis if not for the fact that the works analyzed with respect to these databases contain the same narrow focus.

226 Willy Peremans and E. van't Dack, *Prosopographia Ptolemaica* (10 Vols.; Lovanii: Bibliotheca Universitatis, 1950–2002).

227 This covers only statistically valid entries, following Bauckham's meticulous analysis (*Jesus and the Eyewitnesses*, pp. 69–71).

228 Jonathan Reed, "Instability in Jesus' Galilee: A Demographic Perspective," *JBL* 129.2 (2010), pp. 343–365, esp. 348, 353–54; McIver, *Memory*, pp. 189–209.

229 David Schaps, "The Woman Least Mentioned: Etiquette and Women's Names," *Class Q* 27.2 (2009), pp. 323–330, esp. 330.

230 Ilan I, pp. 3, 11.

231 M. B. J. Keurentjes, "The Greek Patronymics in -(ί)δας / -(ί)δης," *Mnemosyne* 50.4 (1997), pp. 385–400, esp. 386.

232 The patronym can also serve as nickname (Ilan I, 18), a phenomenon supported by NT transliterations (cf. Σίμων Βαριωνᾶ, Matt. 16.16). For thorough treatments: Ilan I, pp. 32–34; Bauckham, *Jesus and the Eyewitnesses*, pp. 83–84.

233 Benet Salway, "What's in a Name? A Survey of Roman Onomastic Practice from c. 700 B.C. to A.D. 700," *The Journal of Roman Studies* 84 (1994), pp. 124–145, esp. 125.

234 Ibid., p. 125.

235 Ibid., p. 126.

236 Ibid., p. 130.

237 This point can be overemphasized, since Jewish persons bearing this

theophoric name are attested in Palestine, albeit rarely and after 70 CE (e.g. Ilan I, p. 281; CIIP III 2179; CIIP IV 3484).

238 The edition consulted for this was Bart D. Ehrman and Zlatko Pleše, *The Apocryphal Gospels: Texts and Translations* (New York: Oxford University Press, 2011).

239 Ilan I, pp. 432–433. Citations for the Gospel of Nicodemus refer to the M. R. James translation, *The Apocryphal New Testament* (Oxford: Clarendon Press, 1924).

240 Citations for the apocryphal Acts refer to the M. R. James translation, *The Apocryphal New Testament*.

241 Number of attestations in the LGPN I–V: Λάμων, *Daphn*. 1.1 (0); Φιλητᾶς, 2.3 (1); Χρομις, 3.15 (0); Διονυφανης, 4.13 (0); Νάπη, 1.6, only attested elsewhere as a Roman name (*Epig. Rom.* di Canosa Add. 21). Citations in this text refer to Jeffrey Henderson's version, *Longus: Daphnis and Chloe / Xenophon of Ephesus: Anthia and Habrocomes* (Cambridge, MA: Harvard University Press, 2009).

242 Two exceptions: Χλόη, *Daphn*. 1.6 (also attested in Charitonides, *Sympl*. 37); Μεγακλής, 4.35 (attested in the seventh century BCE, *Arist*. 1311 b, 27).

243 E.g., Μένων has 275 attestations in the LGPN I–V, but none are attested in the given deme (Messene, *Chaer*. 1.7); Attestations from Lydia in LGPN V5a amount to 11,272, but the name Φαρνακής—allegedly from Lydia (*Chaer*. 4.1) —is unattested there; the rare names Ζηνοφάνης and Μιθριδάτης are qualified (1.7, 3.7), while Διονυσιος, a very common name, is not (1.12). Citations of *The Aethiopica* refer to the version privately printed for the Athenian Society (Athens, 1897), available online at https://archive.org/stream/aethiopica00cologoog#page/n9/mode/1up; retrieved on Dec. 23, 2019.

244 E.g., There are five times more attestations of Χαρμίδης (*Leuc. Clit.* 4.2.1) in the LGPN I–V than in ProsPtol; also, more attestations of Μενέλαος (*Leuc. Clit.* 2.33.1), although this comparison is less significant. Numbers of attestations in the LGPN I–V: Καλλιγόνη, *Leuc. Clit.* 1.3.1 (2 attestations in the LGPN); Λευκίππη, 1.3.6 (3); Κλειοῖ, 1.16.1 (0); Ζήνωνι, 2.17.2 (0); Κώνωψ, 2.20.1 (3); Γοργία, 4.15.1 (2). Μελανθώ, 6.1.2 (4). Citations refer to the text of *Leucippe and Clitophon* (Cambridge, MA: Harvard University Press, 1969).

245 Loveday Alexander, "Fact, Fiction and the Genre of Acts," *NTS* 44.3 (1998), pp. 380–399, esp. 391, 396.

246 The ten qualified names: Cyrus, the Persian (1.1.3); Croesus, the king of Lydia (2.1.5); Artacamas, the king of Greater Phrygia (2.1.5); Aribaeus, the king of Cappadocia (2.1.5); the Arabian, Aragdus (2.1.5); Gadatas, the castrated prince (5.3.10); Andamyas, the Mede (5.3.38); Rhambacas, the Mede (5.3.42); Abradatas, the king of Susa (6.3.35); Pheraulas, the Persian (8.3.2). Citations to *Cyropaedia* refer to the version by Walter Miller in *Xenophon in Seven Volumes* (Cambridge, MA: Harvard University Press, 1914).

247 Cf. *Vita Apoll.* 2.20, 'Porus'; Christopher Jones, "Apollonius of Tyana's Passage to India," *GRBS* 42.2 (2001), pp. 185–199, esp. 192, 197; Krzysztof Nawotka, *The Alexander Romance by Ps.-Callisthenes: A Historical Commentary* (Netherlands, Brill: 2017), pp. 169–183.

248 Nawotka, *Commentary*, p. 173. The in-text citation of *The Alexander Romance* refers to the Greek recension α, ed. by W. Kroll (Berlin: Weidmann, 1926).

249 Τιμασίων, "an Egyptian from Naucratis," has twenty results in the LGPN I–V, with greatest concentrations in Athens, Issa, and Hyettos, but it is attested only singly in Egypt (I. Memnonion 245, 1); Θρασύβουλος, "a native of Naucratis," is attested only twice in Egypt (P. Oxy. 12 1479, Ro 2; I. Hermoupolis 8, 3) in Hermoupolis and Alexandria respectively, but over a hundred times in the LGPN I–V, with concentrations around Athens and Priene; Φιλίσκος is attested over three hundred times in the LGPN I–V but half as much in ProsPtol; Νεῖλος is nowhere attested in Egypt but over thirty times around the Northern Mediterranean; Στρατοκλῆς, "from Pharos," is attested 159 times in the LGPN I–V but under 20 times in ProsPtol; Θεσπεσίων is nowhere attested. In-text citations refer to the edition, *Vita Apollonii*, ed. Carl Ludwig Kayser (Lepizig: Teubner, 1871).

250 Qualified names: Sostratus the Boeotian; Timocrates of Heraclea; Python, son of some Macedonian; Peregrine Proteus; Agathocles the Peripatetic; Cyprian Rufinus; Herminus the Aristotelian (*Demonax*, 1, 3, 15, 21, 29, 54, 56). Citations refer to the text by A. M. Harmon (Cambridge, MA: Harvard University Press, 1913).

251 Despite its focus on the Roman conquest of Britain, only a few named persons are Britons (e.g., Cogidumnus, 14.1; Boudicea, 16.1; Galgacus, 29.4). Citations refer to the edition by Sara Bryant, *The Complete Works of Tacitus* (New York: Random House, 1942).

252 Iulius has 671 attestations in the PIR, 4 in *Agr.*; Caesar has 66 attestations in the PIR, 2 in *Agr.*; Nerva also has 13 attestations in the PIR, 2 in *Agr.*

253 E.g., Βάννους (*Vita* 11) has a single attestation in Ilan I, p. 81; Ἀλιτύρος (16) is unattested; Πιστὸς (34) is singly attested in Ilan I, p. 303; Γόζορος (197) is unattested; Σακχαῖος (239) is only attested in *Vita* with this spelling, but likely derived from Zechariah (cf. Ilan I, p. 90); there are, however, exceptions (e.g. James and Ananias in *Vita* 96; cf. Ilan I, p. 290). Citations of *Vita* refer to the text by B. Niese (Berlin: Weidmann, 1890).

254 Based on Table 7 from Ilan I, p. 56.

255 Publius has 267 (*nomina* 4, *praenomina* 263) attestations in the DPRR from a total of 3478 persons; Publius is attested twice from the 127 persons in *Caesar*; i.e. 1.6% vs 7.7%. Marcus (*praenomen*) has 401 of 3478 vs 3 of 127; i.e., 11.5% vs 2.4%. Cornelius (*nomen*) has 127 of 3478 vs 3 of 127; i.e., 3.6% vs 2.4%. Citations to Plutarch's *Caesar* and *Pompey* refer to the text by Bernadotte Perrin (Cambridge, MA: Harvard University Press, 1919).

256 A sampling of the rarity of unqualified names in *Jul.*: Plotius, 5 attestations in DPRR; Lepidus, 22; Sertorius, 1; Cicero, 8; Axius, 3; Catilina, 2; Vettius, 11; Cato, 10; Scipio, 14; Naso, 9; Curio, 5; Hertius, 2. On common names: Caesar (*cognomen*) has 18 attestations of 3478 persons in the DPRR vs 3 of 144 in *Jul.*; i.e., .5% vs 2%. Silanes (*cognomen*) has 11 of 3478 vs 2 of 144; i.e., .3% vs 1.4%. Aemilius (*nomen*) has 38 of 3478 vs 2 of 144; i.e., 1% vs 1.4%. Marcus (*praenomen*) has 400 of 3478 vs 11 of 144; i.e., 11.5% vs 7.6%. Lepidus (*cognomen*) has 22 of 3478 vs 2 of 144; i.e., 6% vs 1.4%. Cornelius (*nomen*) has 127 of 3478 vs 5 of 144; i.e., 3.6% vs 3.5%. Lucius (*praenomen*) has 517 of 3478 vs 6 of 144; i.e., 14.8% vs 4.2%. Quintus (*praenomen*) has 269 of 3478 vs 7 of 144; i.e., 7.7% vs 4.9%. Citations of Suetonius' *Divas Julius* refer to the text by Alexander Thomson (Philadelphia, PA: Gebbie & Co., 1889).

257 *Pompey* contains reflective patterns similar to *Caesar* and *Julius Divus*. A sampling of qualified and unqualified names, however, further demonstrates how common names are generally qualified in *Pompey* while rarer names are not: the first seven qualified names, for example, are: Philippus (11 attestations in DPRR); Terentius (30); Valerius (46); Aurelius (28); Octavius (33); Calvinus (7); and Lentulus (35). The first seven unqualified names are: Cinna (8); Antistius (14); Carbo (10); Sulla (11); Vedius (1); Carrinas (3); Cloelius (4).

258 Keener, *Christobiography*, pp. 15–18, 33–34, 68, 79–94, 150.

Index

Alexandre, Yardenna, 25, 144

ambiguous image, 82–83, 110

androcentrism, 43–44, 117

Anne Frank (see Frank, Anne)

anonymity, 40, 43

apocryphal Acts, 119–120

apocryphal gospels, 34–35, 118–119

Aramaic, 32, 32, 39, 43, 54

Aristides, Aelius, 48

Augustus, Caesar, 101–103

authentication, 15

authenticity, 32, 36, 42

autopsy, 19, 72

Bailey, Kenneth, 44, 108–109

Bartimaeus, 58, 74–75, 79

Bauckham, Richard, 32, 37, 75

Beloved Disciple, 27, 81, 85–86, 87

biblical language, 26–27, 59–62, 73, 74, 75, 96–97

biographies, Greco-Roman, 34, 36, 41, 43, 110, 121–123

Blomberg, Craig, 54

Bock, Darrell, 88

Bostock, Gerald, 96

Brodie, Thomas, 91–92

Burke, Trevor, 108

Caesarea, 51

Cauda, 49

Christology, 60, 72, 73, 91–110

Cleopas, 58, 61

code-switching, 53

compassion, 109

convergence, 27, 74, 78

corroborative (see evidence)

deception, 16–17, 76

Denaux, Adelbert, 54–55

Derico, Travis, 32, 44

discourse markers, 54–55, 61, 75

divinity, of Jesus, 102–103, 104–105, 107–110, 113

Dow, Sterling, 46

Dunglish, 40

Edwards, James, 40, 55

Elijah, 91–97

Elisha, 91–97

evidence, 18, 22, 26

corroborative, 20–21, 28–29, 82, 112–113

Fellows, Richard, 23–24

Fitzmeyer, Joseph, 71–72

Frank, Anne, 27, 63–70, 76, 78–79

Gilchrist, John, 48–49

Gill, David, 45, 88

Gospel differences, 43

Gospel of John, 27, 29, 75–76, 81, 82–86, 87, 90, 96–97, 99, 107–110

Gospel of Mark, 29, 39, 62, 71–81, 88, 95, 106

Gospel of Matthew, 29, 39, 44, 71, 75–76, 80, 84–85, 95

Great Interpolation (see Travel Narrative)

Hemer, Colin, 48

Herod Antipas, 44, 62

Herodotus, 19

historiography, 84

ancient, 19, 72, 77, 86

Greco-Roman, 19–20, 34, 36, 59, 77, 123

historical difficulties, 29

historical explanation, 42, 85–86

limitations, 15

Hogeterp, Albert, 54–55

Holocaust, 27, 31–32, 62, 63–70, 76, 78–79

Hornblower, Simon, 32

house churches, 51

Ilan, Tal, 32

Infancy Narrative, 59–60

inquiry, 19, 74

interconnectedness, 80, 82–86, 88, 90, 96–97, 99–100, 107–110

interpreters, eyewitnesses as, 61

James, brother of Jesus, 44, 46–47, 143

James, son of Zebedee, 39, 43, 72, 87–88

Jesus, depiction of (see Christology)

Jesus and the Eyewitnesses, 37

Joanna, wife of Chuza, 44, 58, 62, 76, 80

John, son of Zebedee, 39, 43, 72, 87–88

John the Baptist, 103, 104

Johnson, Luke Timothy, 71

Josephus, 26, 35–36, 42, 71, 73, 122

Keener, Craig, 36

kerygma, 84

Kingdom of God, 102

L material, 40

Lake Gennesaret (see Sea of Galilee)

Lamar, Cribbs, 85

literary creativity, 21, 61, 77, 79–80, 88, 96, 101–103, 106–107, 149

Lucian, 48

Luke, as traveling companion of Paul, 28, 47, 51, 87

Marincola, John, 20

Markan priority, 39, 77–78

Mary Magdalene, 76

Mary, mother of James, 76

Mary, mother of Jesus, 23–24, 59–61, 100–102, 114

McGrew, Lydia, 80

McIver, Robert, 50–52

memory, 30, 50, 64–65, 69–70

Menken, Maarten, 109

miracles, 29

mnemonics, 43

names

of persons, 22, 27, 30–47, 50, 62, 77, 79–80, 87, 111–112, 115–123

of places, 48–49, 72–73

theophoric, 46

nautical jargon, 49

Nazareth, 25

novels, ancient, 120–121

onomastic congruence, 34, 36, 37, 42, 45, 47, 61, 115–123

onomastics, 32

oral tradition, 42–45, 86

Osiek, Carolyn, 43

Parker, Pierson, 84

patterns, 16, 22–23, 24, 26, 27, 29, 34–35, 37, 39, 45–47, 61, 81, 149

Peter (see Simon Peter)

Peters, John, 19

Pliny, the Elder, 49

Plutarch, 35–36, 42, 48, 59, 78, 122–123

Pontius Pilate, 99–100

primitivity, 43, 97

prologue, of Luke, 18–19, 54, 60, 87, 90

prosopography, 33, 35, 116

Protevangelium of James, 33

redaction, 43, 62, 65, 71–75, 78–79

Reiser, Marius, 48

reliability, 54

Riesner, Rainer, 45, 87–88

Robertson, J.A., 89

Roman imperialism, 26–27, 101–103, 111–114

sailing, 49

Salome, 76

scroll, 7, 26

Sea of Galilee, 72–73

Semitism(s), 23–24, 39–40, 43, 46–47, 52, 53–61, 73, 74, 75, 88, 124–139

Septuagint, 26, 96

shipwreck, 28, 48, 50–51

Sign Prophets, 97

Simon Peter, 44, 46–47, 55–58, 60–61, 71–74, 79, 87–88, 104–105

Stark, Rodney, 51

Strickland, Michael, 33, 115

Suetonius, 35–36, 42, 123

sycamore, 75

synagogue servant, 61

Synoptic Gospels, 39, 41, 82, 84

tell, 7, 15–16, 18, 22, 28–29, 35–36, 38, 80–81, 98, 110, 112–113, 149

temple, 107–108

The Twelve, 43

tip-of-the-tongue, 30

theography, 110

Thucydides, 19, 21, 45, 52, 74

toponyms, 48–49, 73–74

transfiguration, 59, 88

trauma, 50

travel, 19, 52, 89–90, 92–93

Travel Narrative, 88–97

tria nomina, 117–118

truth telling, 16, 76, 112

undesigned coincidences, 80–81, 99–100

unity of Luke and Acts, 7, 16

variability, in memory, 65, 69–70, 74, 76, 77, 78–80

vividness, 50–51, 61, 78–79, 85

voyage to Rome, 48–51

"we" passages, 47–52, 60–61, 87, 90

Weeden, Theodore, 44

Williams, Peter, 37–38

women at the tomb, 58, 75–76, 77

Yahweh, 103, 105, 110, 113

Zacchaeus, 58, 75

You Might Also Like

Testimonies to the Truth
Why You Can Trust the Gospels

Christians should be prepared to defend and share their faith, even while wrestling with doubts and questions that arise from within and without. With thousands of books out there—not to mention content on social media—where do we start? *Testimonies to the Truth,* Lydia McGrew's fourth book on New Testament reliability, provides a great starting point. With a heart for evangelism, equipping believers, and scholarship, McGrew brings together new arguments and old ones in a form that is readily accessible to laymen while being careful and rigorous. With these arguments in hand, you will never be stumped when someone asks, "Why should I believe what the Bible says about the life and teachings of Jesus?" Above all, McGrew points to Jesus himself, true God and true man, the One who teaches, loves, and suffers for us, described by the Gospels in vivid and credible detail. ($15.99)

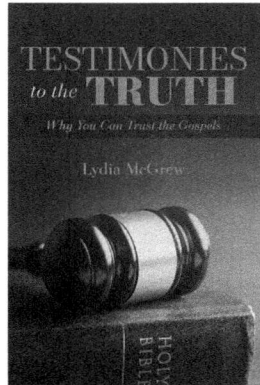

*For a full listing of DeWard Publishing
Company books, visit our website:*

www.deward.com

DeWard™
for your journey